W9-CJR-065

DETROIT PUBLIC LIBRARY

3 5674 00874154 9

DETROIT PUBLIC LIBRARY

CONELY BRANCH
4600 Martin
Detroit, MI 48210

DATE DUE

APR 0 1 1993

MAY 1 8 1994

AUG 3 1 1995

JUN 0 3 1996
JAN 2 1 1997

THE BEGINNER'S GUIDE TO AMERICAN BONSAI

THE BEGINNER'S GUIDE TO
AMERICAN BONSAI

JERALD P. STOWELL

with a foreword by
KYUZO MURATA

KODANSHA INTERNATIONAL LTD.
Tokyo, New York, and San Francisco

635.965
S893b3
c. 1

Distributed in the United States by Kodansha International/USA, Ltd. through Harper & Row, Publishers, Inc., 10 East 53rd Street, New York, New York 10022. In South America by Harper & Row, International Department. In Canada by Fitzhenry & Whiteside Limited, 150 Lesmill Road, Don Mills, Ontario M3B 2T6. In Mexico and Central America by HARLA S. A. de C. V., Apartado 30-546, Mexico 4, D. F. In the United Kingdom by Phaidon Press Limited, Littlegate House, St. Ebbe's Street, Oxford OX1 1SQ. In Europe by Boxerbooks Inc., Limmatstrasse 111, 8031 Zurich. In Australia and New Zealand by Book Wise (Australia) Pty. Ltd., 104-8 Sussex Street, Sydney 2000. In the Far East by Toppan Company (S) Pte. Ltd., No. 38, Liu Fang Road, Jurong, Singapore 22.

Book design, typography, and layout of illustrations by Rebecca M. Davis.

Published by Kodansha International Ltd., 2-12-21 Otowa, Bunkyo-ku, Tokyo 112 and Kodansha International/USA Ltd., 10 East 53rd Street, New York, New York 10022 and 44 Montgomery Street, San Francisco, California 94104. Copyright in Japan 1978 by Kodansha International Ltd. All rights reserved. Printed in Japan.

LCC 77-15372
ISBN 0-87011-326-7
JBC 2076-786308-2361

First Edition, 1978

MAY '79

CONTENTS

FOREWORD

IN the spring of 1967 seventeen members of the Bonsai Society of Greater New York came to Japan to study the art of bonsai with me for a week at my bonsai garden. Among the members of that group were Jerald Stowell, the first president of the Bonsai Society of Greater New York, who was then serving as president, and Mrs. Lynn Perry Alstadt, who is now executive secretary of the American Bonsai Society, of which Mr. Stowell was also first president.

At the time of that first seminar, Mr. Stowell had already created numerous bonsai and the questions he asked me were quite different from those posed by others in the group. I recall that at the second bonsai seminar, in 1971, Mr. Stowell's astute questions verged on the professional. In the summer of 1975, when I flew to the United States to give a series of lectures in various parts of that country, I saw Mr. Stowell for the first time in several years and learned that he was planning to publish a second book on bonsai. At that time I asked him rather detailed questions about the contents of his forthcoming book. Then when Mr. Stowell came to Japan in October, 1977, he told me that *The Beginner's Guide to American Bonsai* was ready to be published.

I have been most impressed by Mr. Stowell's attitude in writing this book. It is common for an author to take two or three years to write a book, but Mr. Stowell spent fifteen years refining his work. Each time we met after an interval of several years, I discovered that his thoughts about the creation of bonsai and how to appreciate the art form had deepened and become much more innovative.

Although this book is intended for the beginner, Mr. Stowell has included information of value not only to the beginner but to the professional bonsai cultivator, as well. His chapters on the design principles of bonsai and creating a good soil mixture are especially useful.

The most important consideration in a book on bonsai should be the area to which the information applies. In the case of Japanese books on bonsai, the district covered usually centers on Tokyo and its environs, and recommendations for pruning, soil mixtures, and so forth are stated rigidly. Therefore, Japanese books on bonsai, which are adapted to the soil and climate of central Japan, will be of little use in a country like the United States. In North America, a book written by an experienced resident bonsai cultivator will be the best reference work.

Mr. Stowell's chapter on regional variations in caring for bonsai, with its specific recommendations for regional adaptations, is an extremely important contribution to American bonsai literature. To my knowledge, no other book on bonsai addresses the problem of the vast regional differences in care and materials that quite naturally exist on a continent as large as North America. This chapter, along with appendixes C, D, and E, will be of immeasurable value to bonsai cultivators in North America.

To write this book, Mr. Stowell, who currently lectures on bonsai at Temple University in Philadelphia and at Brookdale Community College in Lincroft, New Jersey, has drawn on his rich knowledge of bonsai and his long experience in the field. I am certain that *The Beginner's Guide to American Bonsai* will contribute to increased interest in bonsai not only in North America but throughout the West.

I heartily congratulate Mr. Stowell on his achievement; the fruits of his enthusiasm will benefit many readers.

KYŪZŌ MURATA
Kyuka-en
Omiya Bonsai Village

AUTHOR'S PREFACE

WRITERS in both Japan and the West have produced numerous books containing a wealth of technical information about the methods used in growing bonsai in Japan. For the most part these books discuss Japanese horticultural materials (with their Japanese names) and style classifications, as well as the use of Japanese soil and tools. The technical information is well presented and is valuable to anyone who wishes to study this traditional art form. In general, however, these books seldom explain the rationale for the various methods and techniques.

During the past twenty years I have tried to apply these methods and techniques in developing bonsai in America. At the same time I have tried to analyze why they are successful in Japan and to determine how they can be adapted for use in North America, where the climate is characterized by great extremes and variations from north to south and east to west.

This book has been written as a guide for the beginner, to explain why certain methods and techniques have worked for me and to explain how numerous methods and techniques were adapted to suit the climatic conditions in my area of America. If a beginner has not been able to study bonsai with a Japanese master or has not visited Japan, it is difficult for him to develop bonsai by trial and error unless he has some understanding that bonsai is a horticultural art form and not just a tree or shrub in a flowerpot. Once the methods, techniques, and art form are understood, there is no reason that bonsai cannot be developed and appreciated by the amateur gardener or hobbyist, since adaptations can be made to accommodate local conditions.

For their invaluable help during the past year while I was preparing this book for publication, I am indebted to: Roslynde T. Steinig and Helene T. Bertino for typing the manuscript; Charles L. Maddox for his skill in taking the color photographs; George W. Baker for much valuable information on soil mixtures; Dorothy Ebel Hansell, editor of the American Bonsai Society's publication, *Bonsai Journal,* for permission to quote material printed in the *Bonsai Journal;* and the Pennsylvania Horticultural Society and the Rosade Bonsai Studio for permission to use photographs taken at the Philadelphia Flower and Garden Show.

I am highly honored that Japan's leading authority on bonsai, Mr. Kyūzō Murata, of Kyuka-en, Omiya, has written the foreword to this book; and I am delighted that it is being published first in Japan, the home of bonsai.

Finally, I am most grateful to Warren P. Cooper for the use of his black and white photographs in order to compare the development of certain bonsai over a twenty-year period and for his patience during the completion of my second book.

THE BEGINNER'S GUIDE TO
AMERICAN BONSAI

1. INTRODUCTION

FOR thirty years or more, the Japanese word "bonsai" has been known in America, but its technical meaning is still generally unfamiliar to most people. The essence of bonsai lies in techniques applied to horticultural material, not in the plants themselves; however, we apply the word bonsai to the trees or shrubs trained in stylized forms and grown in special containers. Pressed for a definition, we might say that a bonsai is a three-dimensional, living art-form. Bonsai is a creative work, since one takes plant materials and by specialized techniques reshapes them into beautiful, living, miniature trees. Through these techniques and with the application of principles of design, the plants are developed into objets d'art. In maturity a bonsai is something of nature evoked in miniature. It is to be appreciated in the home or garden as a piece of sculpture, which indeed it is.

For the past ten years several of Japan's leading bonsai teachers have toured throughout the United States giving demonstrations at various meetings and symposia on the techniques of developing bonsai from materials grown in America. Because of their presence and because of the numerous English-language books on the subject, two new words have been introduced into the vocabulary and must be defined and explained. These terms are *saikei* and *suiseki*. Saikei is defined as "plant view," or a scenic view expressed with living plant materials and stones arranged artistically in a pottery tray. Suiseki is defined as "water stone," or a scenic view expressed with stones arranged artistically in a pottery or bronze tray. Stones are selected to represent scenes in nature, such

2. Near the seashore, this unusual eastern red cedar, *Juniperus virginiana*, has been shaped by the wind.

1. The typical shape of the American white pine, *Pinus strobus*.

3. Also near the seashore, this wax myrtle, *Myrica cerifera*, too, has been shaped by the wind.

as a distant mountain or an island in the sea. They can be displayed in a tray with water, on wet sand, or on dry sand. When displayed on a wooden stand as a dry stone, the suiseki is shown indoors. These various art forms are being practiced and enjoyed by many Americans today as we become more aware of our own natural scenery and adapt the Japanese techniques for our own use and pleasure.

Originally the art form of bonsai was strictly Japanese. The first teachers came from Japan or were of Japanese descent, and to teach their students in the United States they used domestic plants or plants imported from Japan as prototypes of bonsai. Eventually, American nurseries began to propagate plants from seeds and cuttings in order to supply students and customers with the Asian species commonly used in Japan for bonsai. Yet, the early enthusiasts in America felt they did not possess a true bonsai unless the bonsai was an exotic plant, such as *kuro-matsu, Pinus thunbergii,* the Japanese black pine; or *goyō-matsu, P. parviflora* var. *pentaphylla,* the Japanese five-needled pine; or *buna, Fagus crenata,* the Japanese beech.

Nurseries also imported tools, containers, and mature bonsai from Japan for

Field-grown trees have unmistakable characteristics that can be recognized instantly.

4. Spruce.

5. Locust.

6. Hickory.

7. Eastern red cedar.

8. Pin oak.

9. Elm.   10. Apple.

resale to an ever-expanding American public that knew bonsai only as a Japanese art.

In the past, the acknowledged bonsai were Japanese, and the stylistic rules that the Japanese developed reflected the view of nature held in the Orient. As we did with flower arrangement, we are now developing American styles of bonsai. The styles, based on the traditional Japanese styles, are gradually being changed to reflect our own view of art and, most particularly, of nature. Today the serious students of bonsai are collecting from the wild and discovering that plants native to America have as handsome possibilities for bonsai as do the Asian varieties.

Many native plants are now being used for bonsai, such as the American bald cypress, *Taxodium distichum,* found in the South; the cedar elm, *Ulmus crassifolia,* found in Texas; the California juniper, *Juniperus californica,* found in California; the alpine fir, *Abies lasiocarpa,* found in the Northwest; to name just a few around the country. In the Northeast and temperate areas of America such species as the eastern red cedar, *Juniperus virginiana,* which makes an excellent bonsai, are being used. Trained to its natural form, the eastern red cedar could become the American oval shape with driftwood effect. The Chinese juniper, *Juniperus chinensis,* grown in the informal upright style with driftwood effect would be comparable, but by no means a counterpart.

With its brilliant fall color and gray-white bark, the American red maple,

11. Oak.　　　　　　　　　　　　　　　12. Willow.

Acer rubrum, makes a most attractive bonsai. I have appreciated one of these maples in a container for ten years. So grown, the plant gradually produces smaller leaves and is sturdy enough to be leaf-trimmed each year. In spring the branch tips turn red just before the leaf buds open. In maturity it is naturally upright with a layering of leaves that forms an irregular oval that is most pleasing. As a bonsai, this maple might introduce an American oval shape.

I have collected a variety of *Acer rubrum* that grows in the New Jersey Pine Barrens and like it for bonsai because the leaves are smaller. This tree looks very like the Japanese trident maple, *Acer buergerianum.*

The native white pine, *Pinus strobus,* has a magnificent adult form that could be trained to an American informal upright shape. The Japanese *goyō-matsu* is similar but not a counterpart. The American pitch pine, *Pinus rigida,* could replace the similar Japanese black pine. The native winterberry, *Ilex verticillata,* is similar to *umemodoki,* the deciduous Japanese holly, *Ilex serrata.*

As we study these and other native trees in their natural environment, our artistic view of bonsai is being altered and our bonsai will be miniature reflections of American elms, maples, apples, and pines. The culture and training required to develop these native plants into bonsai are the same as those for the Japanese plants, and perhaps bonsai developed from native plants are more deeply gratifying to us.

2. THE PRINCIPLES
OF BONSAI DESIGN

BONSAI is a creative work. One takes plants or plant materials and by specialized techniques reshapes them into beautiful, living, miniature trees: an art form that is part horticulture and part artistry—both must be present if a bonsai is to become a work of art and not just a potted plant.

In order to have a basic understanding of the subject we need a definition of art, as well as of the basic elements of design. *Webster's New World Dictionary of the American Language* defines art in part as "the human ability to make things; creative work or its principles; making or doing of things that display form, beauty, and unusual perception: art includes painting, sculpture, architecture, music, literature, drama, the dance, etc."

Bonsai is a plastic art, organic and growing, and should contain the basic elements of design inherent in any plastic art, such as form, line, texture, space, and color. Each of these elements is important in the development of bonsai, and each term should be understood in its application to the design of each bonsai.

Form is the shape or outline of a figure, a structure, or any other thing, the particular characteristic that gives each its own identity or appearance. Due to genetics, all species of trees and plants have their own particular form. Typical tree forms are best seen both in isolated field specimens and in group arrangements occurring in a forest. The forms or characteristics found in each of these situations are reflected in single or group plantings of bonsai.

A line can set a boundary, act as a division between qualities, or represent an outline or contour. Lines set limits. The lines of a container set a limit. The person developing bonsai must learn to select or develop materials that will fit into a limited space. The outline of a single tree or of a forest composition has a definite contour that gives character to the bonsai, as well as setting limits to the overall design.

Texture, according to *Webster's New World Dictionary,* is "the arrangement of the particles or the constituent parts of any material, as wood, metal, etc., as it affects the appearance or feel of the surface; the structural quality of a work of art, resulting from the artist's method of using his medium." Bonsai have texture, that of bark and of leaves or needles—smooth, rough, sawtooth, irregular, regular, flat, or round. Deciduous leaves are sometimes combined with evergreens for contrast in texture. Certain species of trees are selected for bonsai because of the texture of their bark, leaves, or needles. The underplanting or ground cover used under bonsai is selected for its texture, as well as its color, to complement the individual specimen. The bonsai grower must select his materials carefully so they possess all these qualities.

Space, in the words of *Webster's New World Dictionary,* is "the continuous expanse extending in all directions or in three dimensions, within which all things exist, thought of as boundless; the distance, expanse, or area between, over, within, etc., things." Space is used in bonsai as the distance between trees in a group or forest planting, or the space that surrounds a single tree in a container. Space is one of the most important elements in bonsai composition. Although the placement of bonsai in a container is dictated in most books, the rationale rarely is given.

Color, states *Webster's New World Dictionary,* is "the sensation resulting from stimulation of the retina of the eye by light waves of certain lengths; vivid quality or character." All plants have this quality—it distinguishes one tree species from another. Color can be that of spring, summer, or fall, or the stark bareness of winter. In bonsai, color is found in the flowers, needles, and leaves, as well as in the bark.

Now that the guidelines or terms of an art form have been defined and briefly discussed, attention should be given to the principles of design that serve as guideposts in the implementation or rendering of a work of art, be it painting, sculpture, or bonsai. These principles of design—balance, rhythm, emphasis, and unity—guide the artist in the creative process of developing any art form, including bonsai.

Balance, whether symmetrical or asymmetrical, implies stability. Asymmetrical balance is a quality that the Japanese seek in their bonsai. Symmetrical balance is often boring and fails to excite the eye. This aspect of design is not thoroughly understood by most Americans unless they have studied art in any one of its forms.

Rhythm implies ordered repetition, an undulating line that leads the eye quietly from its beginning to its end. This is important in bonsai because the eye must not dwell on either just the tree or just the container. The eye must move back and forth or be led gently from the beginning to the end. The eye, traveling around the bonsai, views the overall shape and does not rest on one spot too long. The eye must be comfortable in following the line and not dart back to a specific detail. It must see detail but not be glued to it.

Emphasis gives prominence to a particular form or area. Emphasis can be achieved through strength of line, through depth of color, through light, or through greater detail in one area than in another. One part of a design may be emphasized by contrast in size. Emphasis is achieved in bonsai through contrast in size of trunk, limbs, and twigs; through contrast in size of needles or leaves; through the texture of bark; or through the color of the surface plantings.

Unity uses color, line, form, texture, or space to give a satisfying sense of relationship—everything fits together.

To use the principles of design effectively, the artist must have an idea to express, a direction or objective in mind, something to communicate to the viewer.

An awareness of nature and an understanding of horticultural practice equip today's designers, artists, and craftsmen of bonsai to produce an art that not only reflects the spirit of nature but has the qualities inherent in works of art. Bonsai must reflect the elements of art and the principles of design. Look to nature as the teacher and do not slavishly copy bonsai from pictures. Know the potentials and limitations of the materials you select for bonsai. As the bonsai grower works, he must constantly analyze and evaluate to see if the composition has character, captures the illusion of nature, and is indeed a work of art.

Almost any woody or semiwoody plant can be grown as a bonsai. The commonly used species, however, are those with small leaves or needles so that trunk, branches, twigs, leaves, and roots will be in scale in the overall composition.

Bonsai are meant to communicate an illusion of nature, perhaps a wind-swept tree clinging to a rocky crag; an isolated pine that has survived years of wind, sun, and rain; a stand of such trees; or a lovely distant landscape. Bonsai should never appear grotesque or unnaturally distorted; they should simply suggest nature.

The elements of a bonsai can be broken down into basic components—surface roots, trunk, branches and twigs with leaves, container—all these components should be related in an artistic whole, as with the elements of any other art form.

In developing a bonsai the characteristics of the tree are determined first; then the receptacle is selected. The container functions like the frame for a painting, defining the limits of the composition and emphasizing its identity. The container must not compete with, but enhance, the bonsai, otherwise the illusion is lost.

IMPORTANCE OF THE TRUNK

The trunk is the most important design component of a bonsai; the other aspects of the tree, such as the major branches, secondary branches or twigs, and the leaves, are developed in terms of it. The classical category of single-trunk trees is divided into five basic styles—formal upright, informal upright, slanting, semi-cascade, and cascade—based on the line of the trunk. Japanese artists have followed this classification consistently. The line of the trunk dictates to a degree the nature of the composition. One reason for this is the stiffness of the wood. Sometimes drastic pruning and wiring can change the shape of a trunk, but in old trees or naturally dwarfed material the design may already be permanently set. The only choice left to the grower is the angle of the trunk as it is positioned in the container.

Differentiation of trunk shapes reflects the way trees grow in nature. Light, wind, moisture, and soil determine the shape of the trunk; and trees growing under similar conditions develop in much the same way, except of course for inherent differences in seed variation and species.

After reviewing the numerous texts written by the Japanese, we find that most authorities agree on the five basic styles for individual bonsai. Several authorities state that these styles were inventions of the early part of the twentieth century. Since bonsai is modeled after nature, perhaps these styles also developed from observation of tree forms. "There are certain tree species that have characteristics that distinguish one species from another. These unmistakable characteristics can be recognized instantly by almost anyone, even by people who have never seen

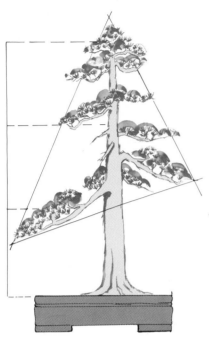

14. The tree is placed off center about two-thirds along the length of the container to allow the longest branch to lie directly above the greater surface area. The shorter branch lies over the remaining surface area.

13 (left). The classic proportions of the formal upright style are the basis for all bonsai. The trunk design is divided roughly into thirds. The lowest third is open: only the trunk and surface roots invite the eye. The middle third (with some open spaces that reveal portions of the trunk as it tapers toward the apex) emphasizes the structure of the branches. In the upper third, the main branches divide into fine branchlets and, finally, into a network of twigs.

certain trees before. Some examples might be the black locust—old trees have an unmistakably stark and gaunt silhouette and look as if they had been shelled in a war; massive, pole-like trunk and main limbs with disproportionately short branches; dark, deeply furrowed, diamond-patterned bark. The pin oak—the only oak whose lower branches almost always are angled downward. The weeping willow—long, slender branches hang straight down like long hair, often touching the ground."[1]

If one observes conifers that grow in North America, such as spruce, fir, and some pines, one will notice that the trunk is usually single, polelike, rising straight out of the ground and continuing, visible and unbroken, to the top of the tree. The characteristics of spruce, fir, and pine seem to be the model for the formal upright style.

FORMAL UPRIGHT STYLE

The formal upright style, with a straight trunk, is essentially a conical, sometimes rounded, tree with an erect leader, or dominant stem, and its lowest branches on a horizontal plane. Frequently, though not always, foliage is contained roughly

1. Andreas Feininger, *Trees* (New York: The Viking Press, 1968), p. 41.

16. Cedar elm, *Ulmus crassifolia*. Informal upright style; height, 27″ (68.6 cm.). Collected material grown as a bonsai about ten years. Owned by the Rosade Bonsai Studio, New Hope, Pennsylvania.

15. California juniper, *Juniperus californica*. Formal upright style; height, 48″ (121.9 cm.). Collected material grown as a bonsai about ten years. Owned by the Rosade Bonsai Studio, New Hope, Pennsylvania.

within a triangle: the apex is the top of the tree, while the two lower angles are formed by the ends of the left and right bottom branches. One of these branches is lower than the other and extends a little farther from the trunk. This style is most often found in coniferous bonsai.

Because deciduous trees usually have several stems or branches competing for adequate light, their growth patterns tend to be irregular. Hence, they are not often used for formal upright bonsai.

In the formal style the tree is usually placed off center about two-thirds along the length of a rectangular container, and just off center from front to back (Fig. 14). The longest branch is usually placed over the greater surface area, while the shorter branch occupies the remaining one-third of the surface area. The shorter branch is usually higher on the trunk than the longest branch and its extremity is closer to the edge of the container. Another branch; usually between the long and short branches in height, extends out to the back of the bonsai for depth.

INFORMAL UPRIGHT STYLE

The informal upright style tends to be an upright tree with a prominent leader; however, its trunk is usually slightly irregular and the apex is curved forward

17. Common apple, *Malus pumila*. Slanting style; height, 15″ (38.1 cm.). Grown from collected material.

18. Natal plum, *Carissa grandiflora*. Semi-cascade style; width, 20″ (50.8 cm.). Grown fifteen years from nursery stock.

toward the front. This style is similar to spreading trees that have trunks that are repeatedly divided and subdivided with trunk and crown merging imperceptibly. This is the growth pattern typical of most broad-leaved trees, such as maple, beech, or oak.

SLANTING STYLE

In the slanting style the trunk bends from the base either to the left or to the right. The trunk may be twisted, curved, or slanted to left or right, with the first or lowest branch growing out in the direction opposite the slant of the trunk. This style of bonsai is usually planted in round or square containers and

19. Juniper, *Juniperus procumbens nana*. Cascade style; length from apex to lowest branch, 42″ (106.7 cm.). Material grown in a nursery twenty-five years from a cutting.

placed slightly off center, with the leader or apex bent toward the front. This style might be found in nature where a tree grows along a stream bed, reaching out for light and competing for a place to grow.

Cascading Styles

Trees that grow in the semicascade and cascade styles might be found in nature growing on the sides of hills, perhaps on a sharp slope, from which they reach out and down, seeking sun and shelter from wind and hard rain. In the semicascade style, the trunk grows up and then curves down at an angle; the tip of the trunk or a major branch dips to a point well below the rim of the container

20 (above left). Japanese hornbeam, *Carpinus japonica*. Forest style; height, 16″ (40.6 cm.); 19″ (48.3 cm.). Owned by the Rosade Bonsai Studio, New Hope, Pennsylvania.

21 (above right). Boxwood, *Buxus sempervirens*. Forest style; height, 18″ (45.7 cm.); width, 18″ (45.7 cm.). Grown fifteen years from three cuttings.

but above its feet on the side toward which the trunk is trained. For balance, a shorter branch is sometimes trained in the opposite direction at a higher level on the trunk.

In the cascading style, the trunk or a major branch usually bends down sharply over the edge of the container, extending well below the feet of the container. However, in some cascade examples the trunk or a branch may be trained upward to form an apex, and a major branch may form the cascade.

OTHER STYLES

In addition to these five basic styles, there are many others, some for groups of trees growing from a single root, some for plantings of multiple trees, some for rock plantings, some for special versions of single-trunk specimens. For those who are interested in more detailed descriptions of the various styles there are numerous books, such as *Bonsai: Miniature Potted Trees,* by Kyūzō Murata, *Bon-*

22 (above left). Japanese maple, *Acer palmatum*. Forest style; height, 22″ (55.9 cm.); width, 21″ (53.3 cm.). Owned by the Rosade Bonsai Studio, New Hope, Pennsylvania.

23 (above right). Pitch pine, *Pinus rigida*. Multiple trunk style; height, 36″ (91.4 cm.); width, 36″ (91.4 cm.). Trained twenty years from three collected seedlings.

sai Techniques, by John Yoshio Naka, and *The Japanese Art of Miniature Trees and Landscapes,* by Yuji Yoshimura and Giovanna M. Halford.

SURFACE ROOTS

Although the trunk is the focal point of and vital to a properly formed bonsai, a well-developed system of surface roots is also necessary. Functionally, roots anchor trees and collect water and mineral salts to be transported through the trunk to the food factories in the leaves. In bonsai, roots have the added *visual* function of giving a tree the appearance of secure placement. Otherwise, confined as it is in a small container, a tree might seem to be toppling over. Woody, tapering surface roots on all sides of the trunk give a bonsai the look of greater stability.

Surface roots also create an illusion of age. Moss growing among roots that radiate from the trunk, with only their surfaces visible, gives the appearance of

24. Pitch pine, *Pinus rigida*. Twin trunk style; height, 30″ (76.2 cm.). Collected twenty years ago as a seedling.

an old, field-grown tree. This effect is lost if roots are drawn so far up that they are *fully* exposed in an unnatural way. Moreover, exposed roots will not thicken and taper as will partially exposed roots.

BRANCHES, TWIGS, AND LEAVES

The branches give a bonsai much of its artistic form—its width and depth. They flow from the trunk and harmonize with it in length and thickness. As it extends out from the trunk, each branch tapers progressively into small twigs.

The design of branches is patterned as closely as possible after that of trees in nature, both young and old specimens, depending on the design being developed. There are considerable design differences between the forms of young and mature trees. Branches near the base of an old tree tend to grow more horizontally than younger branches, which incline to grow upward, as well as outward. In an immature specimen, low, horizontal branches are often entirely lacking. Indeed the branch pattern can be wired and shaped to suggest the image of an aged tree.

Twigs and leaves are the outermost elements of the bonsai. Ideally, leaves are in proportion to twigs, branches, and trunk. Usually, small-leaved plants, such as azaleas and junipers, are chosen, although species with large leaves and interesting configurations of branches and twigs, such as oaks, may be selected for their interesting shape during the dormant period.

In Japan certain deciduous plants are grown as bonsai for their bare winter beauty, as well as for their full summer foliage. The trident maple is an example. This tree develops a fine branch pattern and a twigginess that the Japanese find enjoyable. In the United States, in winter the bark of the American red maple looks silvery gray and the twigs stand out in stark silhouette.

PLACEMENT OF BRANCHES

While bonsai should appear pleasing from all sides, they are composed with a definite front and back, a left and right. The back of the tree is designed to suggest depth, and usually it is the area with the most foliage; this often confuses Westerners, since we like to see masses of leaves all around. The front of a bonsai, however, is kept somewhat open so that the line of the trunk may be clearly seen. Lower branches radiate from the trunk, to left or right, or they may extend toward the back.

The height of a tree and the position of its branches are interdependent. Vertically the upright or slanting bonsai is divided roughly into thirds (Fig. 13). The lowest third is open, only trunk and surface roots show. The middle third emphasizes the structure of the branches, with some open spaces revealing portions of the trunk as it tapers toward the top. In the upper third, the main branches divide into fine branchlets, and finally into a network of twigs.

As a rule, branches radiating from the trunk are arranged in groups of three. Of the three lowest branches, one is trained to the left and one to the right; both trained slightly forward to define the lateral aspect of the tree. To avoid an exact balance, one branch is slightly higher than its counterpart on the other side. The third branch lies on a plane between or above the other two and is trained toward the back for depth.

"The spaces [between branches] should be uneven and wider between the lower branches, and become gradually closer towards the top. In case of too much space, it is better to lower the upper branch instead of raising the lower one."[2]

2. John Yoshio Naka, *Bonsai Techniques* (Santa Monica, Cal.: published for The Bonsai Institute of California by Dennis-Landman, 1973), p. 23.

Each succeeding group of branches is again arranged in a set of three—always with open areas through which the line of the trunk may be seen—until the topmost third of the bonsai is reached. This is usually composed of branches trained toward the front, as well as to the sides and back, so as to form a dense network of fine twigs.

CONTAINERS

Containers are made in various shapes, sizes, colors, and textures; and selection of the proper container depends on the individual tree. Although the form and color of the container are important, neither should detract from the expressiveness of a bonsai. The container should harmonize with the bonsai—complement color and mood—and also be in pleasing proportion to the tree.

Traditionally, there are prescribed colors and shapes of containers for specific types of bonsai. Of course, it is not absolutely necessary to follow Japanese traditions; but since they have been developed to ensure harmony between tree and container, it is usually wise for the beginner not to attempt to innovate at the outset.

Unglazed containers of muted earth tones, such as brown and red, look best with evergreens. Blue, green, or gray glazed containers contrast well with deciduous plants that have orange, yellow, or red flowers or red fruits, as well as with plants that have brilliant fall coloring. Blue is attractive with yellow-flowering trees. Black is excellent with white-berried or white-flowering plants, white to off-white with any other plant. White also looks good with bonsai of a light, airy quality.

A dignified, upright bonsai calls for a flat, rectangular or oval pot of muted color. Slanting trees, too, are usually planted in rectangular or oval pots, though they may be put into round or even square containers. In round or square containers, slanting trees are usually set slightly off center. Trees with thick, heavy trunks and dense foliage look best in dark, sturdy, bulky pots, which contribute to a settled appearance. Shallow, round or oval pots are good for trees with a wind-swept or an informal look. Ornate glazed containers with decorations of flowers or birds are suited to trees that are tall and slim trunked and have delicate foliage. Cascading bonsai are placed in the center of deep pots that are round, octagonal, or square.

3. DEVELOPING BONSAI

MATERIAL for bonsai can be acquired in three ways: one can collect trees from the wild, buy nursery stock, or propagate and grow plants at home. However obtained, material should be well-rooted, well-branched, and sufficiently woody to allow the final form to be clearly defined. It is not true that twenty to thirty years are required to develop a bonsai of quality. If a healthy and vigorous tree is selected, a good bonsai that will live for years can be developed in a few hours. However, the final refinement may take two or three years before the overall design is reached. In Japan many bonsai are started from seeds and cuttings, and it does take many years before they reach maturity as a finished bonsai.

The trunk of the selected specimen should be thick, the surface roots, if exposed, spread evenly around the base, and the branch structure well formed. The leaves should be small, and the twigs, or branchlets, should taper gracefully from the limbs.

The best time to start work on a bonsai is in the spring, at the time that plants emerge from dormancy and rising sap stimulates strong growth, which may continue for a month or more. At this point, a tree is in good condition to withstand the shock of pruning and wiring and to regain health quickly. In most climates, heavy root pruning and potting is safe up to midsummer. In some parts of America where growing seasons are long some species of bonsai may even be potted in the fall.

25. Shown here are the gauges of copper wire most commonly used on bonsai; from left to right the gauges are 8, 10, 12, 14, 16, and 18.

26 (opposite). Of the bonsai tools shown here, some are Japanese and others are American. The basic tools can be purchased at any good garden shop, and substitutions can be made if you cannot obtain the Japanese tools. In the left-hand group the tools are, from left to right: trimming shears, twig nippers, tweezers, combination wire cutter and pliers, and electrician's wire cutter; in the center: turntable with stop and heavy pruning shears; in the right-hand group, from left to right: brush, root hook, rake for soil removal, chopstick, electrician's tape, and tin snips.

SELECTING THE STYLE

The first decision involves the style. Set your tree at eye level and turn it slowly to examine it from every angle. Sometimes the tree itself dictates the style. For instance, a straight-trunked tree is obviously suited to the formal upright bonsai style; a spreading specimen with a hooked trunk might form a natural cascade—the existing trunk line wisely accepted. With other trees there may be a choice. A twisted apple might become either an informal upright or a slanting style. The position of branches may also be a determining factor.

After a style is selected, it is important to determine which side will become the front of the tree. A properly chosen front clearly reveals the line of the trunk and sets the lateral aspects of the bonsai.

Or perhaps it will be the root structure that is the deciding factor in the choice of style. To expose large, heavy roots, dig away some of the soil near the base of the tree with a blunt tool, such as a chopstick. If there are no roots on one side, tilting the trunk may bring some of the lower roots on that side to the surface, thus strengthening the root pattern, but limiting the choice of style.

BRANCH PATTERNS AND WIRING

The next consideration is the pattern of the branches. The three basic branches that should emerge about one-third the way up the trunk are chosen first. All growth below these branches is then pruned away.

Shorten overlong branches, and where branches grow directly opposite each other remove one of them in order to create a proper asymmetrical design. Make clean cuts that leave no stumps so that the bark will heal over the wounds and there will be no scars.

There are exceptions to this rule. When branches need to be eliminated in developing coniferous bonsai, leave the stumps on the tree for one year, since the limb will die naturally and it can then be cut off. Often in conifers pitch will build up where branches have been cut off and large ugly bumps, which are impossible to eliminate at a later time, appear. Some of the dead wood can be left on the bonsai to contribute to the aesthetic effect and add to the illusion of age.

The final design is developed by wrapping copper wire around the trunk and branches and then bending them into position. Annealed copper wire is pliable and easily worked, but it hardens after being twisted, thus holding the trunk and branches securely in place. In time the woody cells of the tree modify and the new positions become permanent.

From a bonsai nursery or hardware store, obtain copper wire in various gauges: 8, 10, 12, 14, 16, 18, and 20. You will probably need the heaviest gauge, 8, for the trunk and main branches and lighter gauges for the branchlets. In each case, select the lightest wire that will serve your purpose. Too heavy a wire may injure the bark; too light may not induce a limb to take the shape you want.

Start wiring at the base of the tree. Anchor a heavy main wire, say, 10 gauge, several inches into the soil at the back of the trunk; then spiral it evenly up and around the trunk. Next, select fairly strong secondary wires, about 14 gauge,

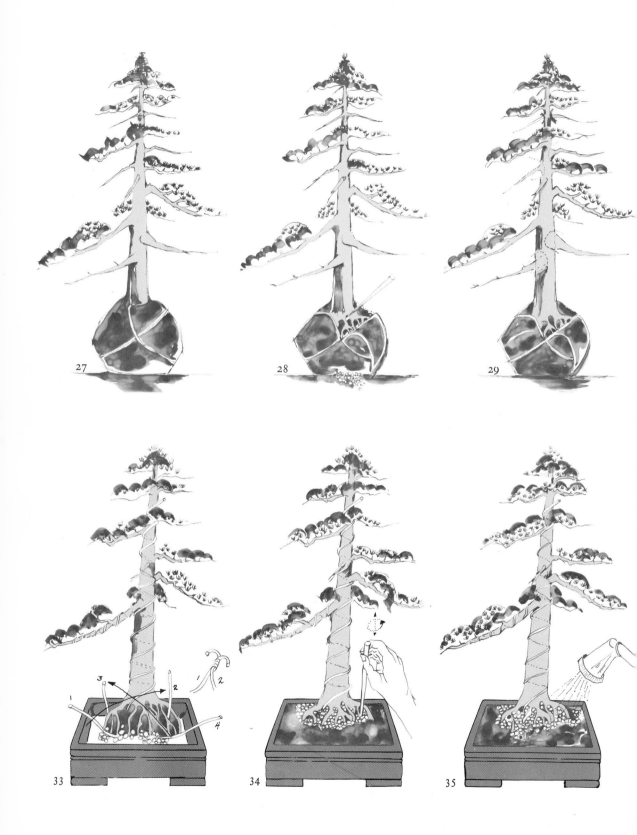

27

28

29

33

34

35

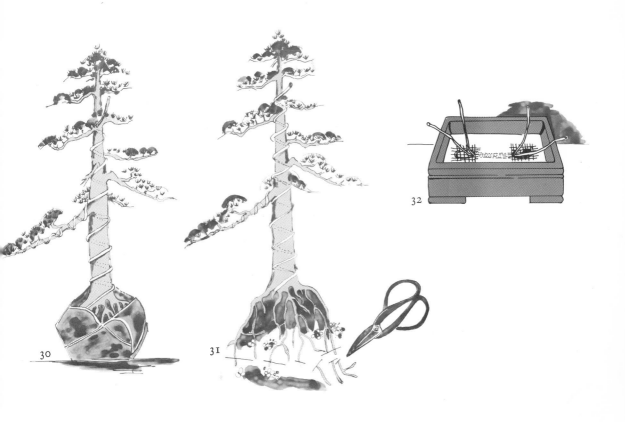

27. A dormant balled-burlaped plant, just before its buds make new growth in spring.

28. Surface roots are exposed by removing soil at the base of the trunk with a chopstick.

29. Preliminary pruning removes opposing branches and reduces the specimen so its main branches will be in scale with the proportions of the composition.

30. Initial wiring sets the basic shape. Copper wire is inserted into the soil and spiraled around the trunk and branches to give the material its artistic shape.

31. The roots are pruned to encourage development of a fine root system.

32. The container is prepared by placing plastic screen over the drainage holes. Copper wire, to hold the tree in place, is inserted through the drainage holes.

33. Bringing wires up through the root ball and securing them by twisting the ends together settles the tree in the container.

34. The main potting soil is worked in and around the roots to eliminate air spaces.

35. The bonsai is watered from above with a fine spray until excess water drains through the holes in the bottom of the container.

and run these around the trunk and out to the tips of the major branches. Use lighter wires, 18 or 20 gauge, for the smaller branches. Pass the side wires around the trunk, but do not attach them to the main wire, since this would look unsightly and would certainly cause bark wounds.

You will be using just one wire for two branches at different levels. In between, wind the wire spirally around the trunk, paralleling but not crossing the main trunk wires. The spiraling may be clockwise or counterclockwise; the spiraling of the wire should follow the direction in which the branch is to be shaped. If spiraled clockwise the branch is shaped toward you, if counterclockwise, the branch is shaped away from you. Wires should be in contact with the branches but not wound so tightly that they interfere with the circulation of sap.

When you get the anchor wires in place, bend each limb into position. Exert a gentle pressure with thumbs and fingers. Gentle is the keyword, no matter how stubborn a branch may be. If you yield to the temptation to force it, you will probably snap the limb, break the cambium layer, just beneath the bark, and so kill the branch.

Some coniferous bonsai should be shaped during their dormant season (see appendixes C and E), while deciduous trees are wired in the early spring, before the new growth appears. If certain plants, such as azaleas, are not watered for two or three days before wiring, they will be more flexible. Be sure to water after the wiring and shaping is accomplished so the plant may recover from this procedure.

Since wires remain on bonsai when they are displayed, neat, unobtrusive wiring is essential, and this takes practice. If you have difficulty at first—everyone does—practice on dead branches instead of on your valued living trees. Soon your fingers will learn the technique, and wiring will become an almost unconscious operation. When you are learning, it may also help to work with heavy twine instead of wire. Twine can be put on and taken off several times without damage to a tree. It is difficult to change a poor pattern worked out with wire, rehearsing with twine is much easier.

SECOND WIRING

How long the first wires are left in place on a potted tree depends on how fast the tree grows. As limbs expand, wires get tight; if they are not removed in time, the bark begins to grow over them. This results in ugly depressions in the wood, sometimes in scar tissue. True, ridges sometimes smooth over and scars disappear, but it takes years. Wiring, therefore, must be watched carefully.

The first wiring will not be sufficient to impose the design on most branches. They will need at least one more wiring, but do not attempt the second wiring until the tree has had a rest. Physiologically this is necessary because wiring in some way alters the cell structure of the bark. Flexing that is repeated too quickly during the growing season can cause a branch to die. Letting a branch remain free of wire for a year can strengthen it; then it can safely be flexed again.

Cell alteration is a slow process, the rate depending on the species, but changes in the cells eventually bring a limb permanently into place. A tree may be considered a mature bonsai when all its branches have been brought to the desired positions and will remain there. Shaping is then only a matter of light pruning. Except for new growth, further wiring is seldom necessary.

PRUNING OF ROOTS

After a tree is shaped and wired for the first time from trunk to twig ends, it is time to cut back the roots. Root pruning stimulates the growth of fine fibrous rootlets. If you reverse the procedure and try to wire *after* potting, you are bound to jostle roots newly set in the soil and perhaps create air pockets there. All this is injurious to pruned roots and likely to result in severe damage or even the death of a plant.

Before you cut the roots, with a blunt tool pry off one-third of the old soil from the root ball. Then cut back the long loose roots one-third. Keep the fibrous filaments attached to larger roots near the trunk because these will sustain the plant while new roots are forming. After root pruning, the plant is ready for potting.

PREPARING THE CONTAINER AND POTTING

Select the container. Then cover the drainage holes in the bottom with small pieces of plastic screen, which prevent soil from escaping but do not interfere with the drainage of water. Next, to stabilize the root ball in the container, from above, insert several lengths of copper wire through one drainage hole. Draw the wires under the pot and up through another hole. If there is only one hole, wrap the wire around a small stick to anchor it to the underside of the pot. To provide good drainage, spread a layer of very coarse sifted soil over the bottom of the container. Over this layer, spread medium-coarse potting soil. Then the container is ready to receive the tree.

Settle the tree in the container with a twisting motion to eliminate air pockets in the soil. Pull the anchor wires diagonally across the root ball and twist the opposite ends together until the tree is firmly set. Then trim off excess wire and push the ends back into the soil. This technique holds the plant exactly where it belongs and ensures against its being dislodged.

Pour in potting soil little by little around the ball of roots. Work it in with a blunt instrument as firmly as you can, to fill up any air spaces. Even a small air pocket around a root can result in an area of rot, and this is particularly dangerous for a newly potted plant.

After the potting soil is well settled, brush away any excess. Sprinkle fine top soil over the entire surface. Even this off and put dry-powdered or fresh moss on top to prevent washing out of soil when the bonsai is watered. You can sprinkle the powdered moss, but fresh moss is first well moistened, then pressed into place with a spatula. It takes time for the powder to become green moss but the fresh moss immediately enlivens the appearance of the tree. Work it in between the roots, always leaving their upper surfaces exposed to give an older look. If you have a variety of mosses and lichens, you can create a miniature landscape under a tree; with the powder, you have to be content with what comes up.

FIRST WATERING

Now it is time for the first watering. Soak the soil well by letting the container stand in enough water to reach just below the rim, and lightly spray the top of the tree. The watering schedule for the next few days is important. If you cut off only a few roots, water again on the second or third day. You can tell when roots begin to take up water again by the dry look of the soil near the trunk. If you have cut off many roots, do not water for several days after the original immersion. Heavily pruned roots are not in condition to absorb much water and are susceptible to rot.

For about three weeks after potting, bonsai need some protection from wind and driving rain. As new growth appears, they can then be treated just as any other bonsai.

4. CARING FOR BONSAI

WATERING is one of the most exacting tasks until a little experience makes it fairly routine. In nature a tree can search far and wide for water; in a container the soil is severely limited. If the soil dries out, a bonsai exhausts its supply of moisture. The necessarily granular type of soil dries out quickly, a circumstance that makes proper watering most important. It cannot be neglected at any time. Contrary to popular opinion, the dwarf character of bonsai is not due to an insufficiency of water, at least not in cultivation.

Bonsai are watered thoroughly almost every day, even in humid weather; only when it rains can the watering of bonsai be omitted. Indeed, in dry and windy weather, bonsai may need to be watered twice a day, since wind causes fast evaporation from leaves. If bonsai are wilted, the leaves should be sprayed with a fine spray before the roots are watered. After spraying the leaves and trunk, then water the roots. Be sure to soak them well and check the plant the next morning to see if it is turgid. Most plants are killed by overwatering and poor drainage. Wilted plants will almost always survive if watered before death occurs; however, once roots are killed because of overwatering, the plant rarely survives.

There are several methods of watering bonsai. If you have time, water them individually with a fine-nozzle watering can or with the fine spray of a garden hose, which may be easier. Either way, each tree must be watered thoroughly. A fog nozzle, available in most lawn and garden shops, does a good job because its spray pressure usually dislodges any insects on the foliage. When you water,

36. Bonsai are watered daily, if necessary, with a fine-spray nozzle attached to a garden hose. The spray is directed toward the container and kept in motion so that water accumulates around the edge of the container but does not wash the soil out. Plants are watered from both sides of the bench so there is uniform wetness until water drains from the container.

notice whether water is coming through the drainage hole of the container. When it does, that is an indication that moisture has saturated the roots and the plant has had enough. My own method is to spray containers in succession until water runs out the drainage hole. Then when all the trees have been watered, I return to the first plant and repeat the process in case one of the plants has not had enough water.

In extremely hot weather, willows and wisteria need an exorbitant amount of moisture. When I leave for business, I place these plants in low, water-filled trays. When I return, every drop of water has been taken up and must be quickly replaced. Other plants that use up water fairly quickly, like miniature bonsai, are best set in sand kept moist in a shallow basin. When it gets cool, toward fall, there is no further need for these precautions and all plants are watered routinely.

SUNLIGHT AND AIR

Sunlight is required for the production of plant food. Insufficient sunlight results in weak foliage and, eventually, a sickly plant that cannot survive. In spring and

37, 38. Kurume azalea, *Rhododenron obtusum*. Cascade style; width, 30″ (76.2 cm.). Trained fifteen years from nursery stock. Twine is wrapped around the trunk to keep the wires from cutting into the bark. Shown in full flower, above, and fall color, below.

39 (top right). Ponderosa pine, *Pinus ponderosa*. Semicascade style; width, 30″ (76.2 cm.). Trained ten years from material collected near Denver, Colorado. This tree needs to have a compact branch structure developed and the size of its needles reduced.

40 (center right). Common apple, *Malus pumila*. Wind-swept style; width, 18″ (45.7 cm.). Trained twenty years from collected material. Accessory plant: woodland aster, *Aster divaricatus*.

41 (below left). Juniper, *Juniperus squamata wilsonii*. Cascade style; width, 20″ (50.8 cm.). Trained twenty years from nursery stock.

42 (below right). Pitch pine, *Pinus rigida*. Multiple trunk style; height, 36″ (91.4 cm.); width, 36″ (91.4 cm.). Trained twenty years from three collected seedlings. This tree needs more pinching to promote compact branching and reduced needle size.

43 (above). Ponderosa pine, *Pinus ponderosa*. Slanting style with drift-wood effect; width, 32″ (81.3 cm.). Trained ten years from collected material. The branches need further development to improve this tree.

44, 46 (right, below right). Common apple, *Malus pumila*. Informal upright style; height, 24″ (61 cm.); width, 36″ (91.4 cm.). Trained twenty years from material collected in the Catskill Mountains.

45 (below left). Southern arrowwood, *Viburnum dentatum*. Informal upright style; height, 27″ (68.6 cm.). Trained twenty years from a col-lected seedling. This tree needs more shaping and pruning to refine its overall shape.

43

47 (above). Pitch pine, *Pinus rigida*. *Bunjin* (literati) style; height, 30″ (76.2 cm.); width, 42″ (106.7 cm.). Trained two years from material collected five years ago.

48 (below left). Juniper, *Juniperus chinensis* var. *procumbens nana,* and azalea. Rock planting style; height, 18″ (45.7 cm.). Trained twenty years.

49 (below right, top). Dwarf crested iris, *Iris cristata*. Tray landscape style. Grown in this container for five years.

50 (below right, bottom). Wildflowers, woodland asters, violets, and various grasses. A grass planting grown five years.

51 (opposite, above left). Ponderosa pine, *Pinus ponderosa*. Twin trunk informal upright style;

height, 36″ (91.4 cm.). The branches should be more horizontal to give the tree a more aged appearance; pinching is continued to encourage dense foliage and reduced needle size.

52 (above right). Austrian pine, *Pinus nigra*. Formal upright style; height, 36″ (91.4 cm.). Developed from nursery stock, with the top cut off and a small branch turned up to develop a new apex. The tree needs fine wiring and shaping to complete the design.

53 (below left). Chinese juniper, *Juniperus chinensis* var. *blaauw*. Formal upright style; height, 30″ (76.2 cm.). Developed from cut-down nursery stock; approximately ten years old. This tree needs wiring and pruning for greater detail.

54 (below right). Japanese black pine, *Pinus thunbergii*. Cascade style; width, 24″ (61 cm.). Developed from nursery stock; thirty years old. Accessory plant: common grass on coral rock.

55 (above left). Gardenia, *Gardenia jasminoides* var. *radicans*. Semicascade style; length, 21″ (53.3 cm.). Material found in a nursery; trained fifteen years. Accessory plant: *Acrous pusillus*.

56 (above right). American elm, *Ulmus americana*. Twin trunk style; height, 36″ (91.4 cm.). Grown twenty years from an air layer.

57 (below left). *Mame* (miniature) bonsai. Main tree: serissa, *Serissa foetida;* secondary tree: geranium, *Pelargonium* sp.; smallest tree: ivy, *Hedera helix*. Grown ten years from cuttings.

58 (below right). Boxwood, *Buxus sempervirens*. Forest style; height, 18″ (45.7 cm.); width, 18″ (45.7 cm.). Grown fifteen years from three cuttings.

59 (opposite, above left). Serissa, *Serissa foetida*. Informal upright style; height, 12″ (30.5 cm.). Grown fifteen years from a cutting. Accessory plant: *Acrous pusillus*.

60 (above right). Mugho pine, *Pinus mugo*. Informal upright style; height, 10″ (25.4 cm.); width, 15″ (38.1 cm.). Grown fifteen years from nursery stock. Originally semicascade, a branch was removed and this tree was restyled in 1976.

61 (below left). Common privet, *Ligustrum vulgare*. Informal upright style; height, 20″ (50.8 cm.). Grown fifteen years from a cutting.

62 (below right). *Mame* (miniature) bonsai. From top to bottom: juniper, *Juniperus procumbens nana*, grown ten years from a cutting; English ivy, *Hedera helix*, grown three years from a cutting; *Acrous pusillus;* woodland aster, *Aster divaricatus*, grown ten years; geranium, *Pelargonium* sp., grown ten years.

63 (above left). *Mame* (miniature) bonsai. From left to right: crab apple, *Malus* sp., grown six years from seed; ponderosa pine, *Pinus ponderosa*, grown five years from seed; *Acrous pusillus*.

64 (above right). *Mame* (miniature) bonsai. From left to right: *Acrous pusillus;* spirea, *Spiraea* sp., grown five years from nursery stock; woodland aster, *Aster divaricatus,* grown ten years.

65 (below left). Juniper, *Juniperus procumbens nana.* Informal upright style; height, 12″ (30.5 cm.); width, 28″ (71.1 cm.). Grown in a nursery twenty-five years from a cutting. Developed into a bonsai four years ago.

66 (below right). American elm, *Ulmus americana.* Informal upright style; height, 28″ (71.1 cm.). Grown fifteen years from an air layer.

67, 68 (above). Common apple, *Malus pumila*. Informal upright style; height, 38″ (96.5 cm.). Collected in western Connecticut in 1957. Detail at left shows branching structure.

69 (below left). Scotch pine, *Pinus sylvestris*. Informal upright style; height, 20″ (50.8 cm.). Grown from nursery stock. Purchased from a friend and restyled in 1977.

70 (below right). Natal plum, *Carissa grandiflora*. Semicascade style; width, 20″ (50.8 cm.). Grown fifteen years from nursery stock. Accessory plant: a succulent, species unknown.

71 (above left). Eastern red cedar, *Juniperus virginiana*. Informal upright style; height, 27″ (68.6 cm.). Grown five years from collected material found along a roadside.

72 (above right). Pitch pine, *Pinus rigida*. Twin trunk style; height, 30″ (76.2 cm.). Collected twenty years ago as a seedling. Rope is wrapped around the trunk to protect the bark while in training.

73 (below). Pitch pine, *Pinus rigida*. Wind-swept style; width, 32″ (81.3 cm.). Collected material.

74 (opposite, above left, top). Dwarf crested iris, *Iris cristata*. Tray landscape style. Grown in this container five years.

75 (above left, bottom). Wintergreen, *Gaultheria procumbens*. An accessory plant.

76 (above right). Boxwood, *Buxus sempervirens*. Informal upright style; height, 27″ (68.6 cm.). Trained four years from nursery stock. The apex needs more growth to complete the design.

77 (below left). Boxwood, *Buxus sempervirens* cv. "Kingsville." Informal upright style; height, 17″ (43.2 cm.). Grown as a bonsai fifteen years from nursery stock.

78 (below right). Kurume azalea, *Rhododendron obtusum*. Informal upright style; height, 20″ (50.8 cm.); width, 30″ (76.2 cm.). Trained ten years from nursery stock.

79 (above left). Juniper, *Juniperus procumbens nana*. Cascade style; length from apex to lowest branch, 42″ (106.7 cm.). Material grown in a nursery twenty-five years from a cutting. Developed as a bonsai four years ago.

80 (above right). European larch, *Larix decidua*. Formal upright style; height, 36″ (91.4 cm.). Grown twenty years from a seedling. Growth is allowed to lengthen and harden before fine wiring is done.

81, 82 (below). Hedge maple, *Acer ginnala*. Informal upright style; height, 40″ (101.6 cm.).

Grown in the ground six years from a cutting before development into a bonsai. Detail shows fine branching structure.

83, 84 (above), 85, 86 (below). Common apple, *Malus pumila.* Informal upright style; height, 24″ (61 cm.); width, 42″ (106.7 cm.). Material collected from abandoned pasture land grown as a bonsai fifteen years. This tree was filled with borer when collected. Above left: detail of borer damage to trunk. Above right: front of tree. Below left: detail showing branching structure from back of tree. Below right: back of tree.

87 (above). Bonsai benches for display and summer care.

88 (below left). Bonsai benches made of redwood posts and fir planks. Twice a year the benches are painted with Cuprinol, a wood preservative, to prevent decay. Height, 34″ (86.4 cm.); width, 24″ (61 cm.); length, 8′ (2.44 m.).

89 (below right). Display stand in a bonsai garden. The stand is made from a chimney flue and

a slab of blue stone. The tree is an Alberta spruce, *Picea glauca conica,* grown on a rock; height, 48″ (121.9 cm.). Ground cover: creeping thyme, *Thymus* sp. Courtesy of the Rosade Bonsai Studio, New Hope, Pennsylvania.

90 (below). A view of the Rosade Bonsai Studio, New Hope, Pennsylvania. The benches are made from chimney flues and fir planks. Courtesy of the Rosade Bonsai Studio.

91 (above). Cold-storage house for winter protection of hardy bonsai in the Northeast during December, January, and February. Cement-block foundation with a fiberglass top. The interior is draped with 4-ply black Mylar to keep the plants dormant and reduce heat on sunny days. The fan draws cold air into the house to keep the inside temperature from rising on sunny days.

92 (below). Cold frame for winter protection and storage. The tops are opened or closed according to the weather. The greenhouse at right is for winter protection of tender bonsai.

autumn, bonsai can stand sun throughout the day, but during the summer heat some deciduous species require protection from direct exposure after two o'clock in the afternoon. The foliage suffers because heat is absorbed by the dark-colored containers, causing damage to the roots, which appears as dark spots or leaf burn. Pines and junipers are an exception, since they prefer drier conditions and should have full sunlight for the entire day.

Sunlight is important for plants, but fresh air is also necessary. Outdoors, air circulating through foliage promotes strong, healthy growth and acts as a deterrent to disease. A strong wind, however, can knock down bonsai, particularly cascading types, and can also tip over containers with narrow bases. To avoid such damage, tie down containers with cord or rubber-jacketed wire, looping it several times around a table and over the tops of the containers. Secure the cord or wire with a sturdy knot to stabilize the bonsai without marring the container.

FERTILIZING

Every bonsai needs enough nutrients to produce foliage of good color—and well-formed flowers and fruit, as well—but not enough to promote excessive growth. Of the many fertilizers I have tried, those containing trace elements, such as Hyponex, Miracle-Gro, or Ra-pid-Gro, are best for bonsai. Ra-pid-Gro has a high nitrogen content and is good for nonflowering plants, where foliage is to be stimulated. All these fertilizers should be diluted to about half the recommended strength.

The important elements in a fertilizer are the macronutrients, such as carbon, hydrogen, oxygen, nitrogen, phosphorus, potassium, calcium, magnesium, and sulfur. The micronutrients are the trace elements, such as iron, manganese, copper, zinc, boron, molybdenum, and chlorine. The six elements that are most important to plants are: nitrogen, which promotes plant vigor and good color; phosphorus, which promotes good root growth and the development of flowers, fruit, and seed; potassium, which promotes root and leaf development and has a role in photosynthesis; calcium, which promotes vigorous growth; magnesium, a constituent of chlorophyll; and sulfur, a constituent of proteins and cell chemistry.

In order for fertilizer to be available to plants, it must be soluble. Plants absorb nutrients through a process of root respiration: nutrient ions close to the root membrane are energized and are transported through the root cell-membrane

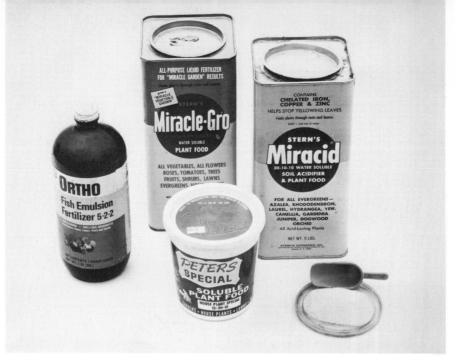

93. The water-soluble fertilizers shown here are suitable for bonsai. From left to right: fish emulsion; Miracle-Gro, for flowering and fruiting bonsai; Peters Special, used in the greenhouse on tender bonsai during winter; Miracid, for evergreen bonsai; powdered limestone (lime crest), granular limestone powder used on plants with more neutral or alkaline soil pH requirements (such as juniper, western pine, or the *Malus* genus).

to the inside of the root. Linked to this vital activity is the interdependence of exhaust from root respiration in the form of carbon dioxide and other organic excretions, since soil microorganisms use these root wastes for their own food and energy supply. The more favorable the soil climate, the easier it is for plants to absorb nutrients and grow. The ideal is soil that is adequately moist at all times, with sufficient quantities of organic matter to provide good pore space and aeration.

There are two kinds of fertilizer: organic, natural materials, such as rape-seed cakes, dried blood, and cottonseed meal; and synthetic, manufactured fertilizers, such as those mentioned above. The organic fertilizer must be broken down into its chemical constituents before a plant can make use of it: plants absorb only pure chemical elements, no matter what the source. Organic materials do have an advantage in that they supply nutrients to the soil over a long period, due to the decomposition process, and are less likely to cause root burn. Inorganic fertilizers are immediately available to the plant. For these reasons some growers use both kinds of fertilizers.

Deciduous plants, such as maples, elms, and hornbeams, are fertilized with a dilute solution each week through the growing season—April to August in northeastern America. Feeding is started just as the trees break into leaf. However, a freshly potted bonsai should not be fertilized for at least a month, until new feeder roots have developed. Young needled-evergreens can be fertilized on

94, 95. Fertilizers are mixed according to the manufacturer's directions and then diluted to half strength with additional water. If the fertilizer is mixed in a wheelbarrow, it can be wheeled to the plants. As the wheelbarrow is moved up and down the rows of plants, each bonsai is submerged in the fertilizer. The gases are allowed to bubble out of the soil, and then the container is picked up, allowed to drain, and returned to the bench.

the same schedule until they reach maturity; then the fertilizer is reduced to once or twice a year, just to maintain the good health of the bonsai and to keep needles small. It is important to remember that excessive feeding will produce excessive foliage, which may be fine for garden plants, but not for bonsai.

IMPORTANCE OF PRUNING

Pruning must be continued the entire life of a bonsai. It is the means by which we keep plants to miniature size, just as shearing a hedge maintains it at the same height year after year. I cannot overstress the importance of pruning, for without it, a bonsai quickly loses form, and the illusion of a miniature tree is lost. Besides keeping a plant small, pruning refines the branch structure into an intricate network of twigs; it also thickens the trunk and forces branch growth where nature may not have intended it. Thus the ultimate form, the aged look, is developed through pruning.

Drastic pruning is usually restricted to the initial potting. But frequently a collector discovers a natural or nursery specimen with a short, well-developed trunk but long, disproportionate branches. These branches must be cut back, no matter how thick they are, if the composition is to develop in scale. On a deciduous tree, new buds soon push through the bark; shoots grow into secondary

branches and, before long, a network of twigs fills in the stark, chopped-off silhouette. If the stub ends of thick branches are carved concave and covered with asphalt, bark will begin to heal over the cut. After a few years the bonsai looks as if it had always been of miniature size.

With evergreens, however, new buds rarely occur. Some species, as pitch pine (*Pinus rigida*), do send sprouts through old bark, but the majority do not. Drastic pruning of evergreens must be a well-thought-out operation.

Sometimes, established bonsai need drastic pruning. After a few seasons a branch may have thickened enough, but the end must go, or perhaps one has second thoughts about style or composition. If surgery is indicated, the time to do it is when the tree is just emerging from dormancy. (For pruning schedules, refer to appendixes C and E.)

Trimming New Growth

Trimming new growth is a different matter. It is repeated every growing season in order to maintain the beautiful shape of fine bonsai. The reason for pruning is to maintain the shape of the bonsai; however, the physiology of pruning is seldom discussed in most texts on bonsai. In order to keep plants healthy and alive over a long period of time, it seems necessary to know some of the facts regarding how pruning affects them.

96, 97, 98. A deciduous bonsai showing new spring growth. Each stem has produced seven or eight nodes. With sharp trimming scissors each stem is trimmed back to one or two nodes. Trimming the bonsai maintains its overall shape and design.

Pruning is a seasonal technique that begins in early spring as the plants become active and is practiced throughout the growing season. In general, early spring growth is made by using food materials produced the preceding year and stored in the plant tissues as sugar, starch, and fat. Only after considerable growth has been made and numerous leaves have developed does a tree or shrub support itself on the current year's food products. The accumulation of food reserves takes place late in the growing season. Thus, if pruning occurs just after stored food has been depleted by developing new tissues and before the stored supplies are replaced, devitalization may be expected to take place. The amount of pruning is a factor: cutting off a large percentage of growth each year will result in a slowing up of growth and food storage and may so weaken the plant that death may occur because of outside causes. This is the reason that drastic pruning is done in the initial stage in the development of bonsai, and if carried out again, it is usually done in the winter or early spring, when the roots are packed with food and strong new shoots will appear in the spring.

Trees respond to pruning in different ways. For example, common privet responds to pruning by producing many new shoots and leaves; *Chamaecyparis* does not tolerate drastic pruning; peaches will withstand heavier pruning than will apples. It is important to learn what the pruning tolerance of your tree is.

Root pruning may be used to slow up vegetative growth and increase flower and fruit production. Many texts point out that flowering and fruiting bonsai should be repotted every two or three years. In these species pruning can influ-

ence the plant's ability to produce flowers and fruit, as heavy pruning and too much fertilization promote vegetative growth and no flowers or fruit.[3]

Fruit spurs on trees of the genus *Malus* (apples and crab apples) normally form on two-, three-, and four-year-old wood. They develop most readily when vegetative growth is reduced. Many bonsai are pruned in late May or June, right after the surge of spring growth. However, to influence apple blossom-bud formation a high carbohydrate supply must be present during the period of bud differentiation—sometime in late June or early July in northeastern America. Therefore, *Malus* bonsai should not be pruned too early in the season or the carbohydrate balance will be upset and no flower buds will appear. Sometimes excessive moisture or dryness will affect flower-bearing trees, causing them to no longer bear blossoms.

When to prune some flowering and fruiting bonsai becomes confusing unless you know whether the flower buds are formed on new or old wood. Certain trees and shrubs that flower before the end of June should be pruned immediately after flowering, as the flower buds have developed on the previous year's growth in the very small form of a bud. Examples of this type of flowering tree or shrub are: the serviceberry, azalea, barberry, bittersweet, redbud, quince, cornelian

3. Everett P. Christopher, *The Pruning Manual* (New York: The MacMillan Company, 1960), pp. 10, 59.

99, 100, 101. A common apple, *Malus pumila,* with long new shoots in the spring. These shoots should be left on the plant for about three months before they are trimmed back to three or four nodes in mid- or late summer. The leaves manufacture starches and sugars necessary to develop flower buds for fruit. If the tree is pruned constantly, it must revert to making new vegetative growth and will not have the strength to develop flower buds.

cherry, hawthorn, privet, honeysuckle, various flowering cherries, plums, and crab apples.

Trees and shrubs that flower after the end of June should be pruned in winter or spring, just before new growth starts, since the flower buds are formed on new wood, as the spring growth develops. Certain trees and shrubs, such as cotoneaster and spirea, may be lightly pruned both before and after flowering.

Some trees and shrubs that are prized for both fruit and flower, such as hawthorn, should be thinned if heavily laden with fruit.

Evergreens, both broad-leaved and narrow-leaved types, may be pruned any time the wood is not frozen. Some deciduous trees, such as maple, dogwood, or elm, that are known as bleeders, due to the heavy flow of sap in early spring, may be pruned in the summer or fall. (See appendixes C and E.)

With deciduous trees each new shoot is allowed to add four or five nodes before it is cut back to only one or two leaves. After a short time, dormant buds break out from nodes farther back on the branch. When a new branch is desired, the shoot is allowed to develop. Little by little, this constant trimming produces the twigginess seen in fine old bonsai.

Needled evergreens grow differently. New growth appears as a pale green bud, or candle, that expands into a cluster of radiating needles. Before it is trimmed, the base of the candle is allowed to become stiff but not woody. Then

102, 103. An evergreen bonsai showing new tip growth. Each new tip is grasped at the base and pinched out with the fingers. If the growth is green and not woody, the tip usually snaps off with little effort. If left too late, however, trimming scissors will be needed when the new growth becomes woody.

with a twisting motion, all but one or two bundles of needles are *pinched* out between the nails of the thumb and the index finger. Needles are *not cut out*. Of all advice, this deserves as much emphasis as I can give it. Cutting new growth on coniferous trees causes browning of the ends, kills back some of the needles that are left, and jeopardizes new bud formation. Always pinch it out.

Trimming at the proper time results in gracefully tapered twigs, but with needled evergreens timing is exceptionally important. Normally, the next year's buds form at the end of the shoot. If the shoot is pinched too late, buds are sacrificed along with it; growth of the limb is effectively checked, as buds will not form if the wood is too old. New buds form on the green wood. They will appear at the end of the pinched-off growth, and the limb will continue its healthy development.

LEAF-TRIMMING

Leaf-trimming is a special kind of pruning that induces dense twigginess in a relatively short time for some deciduous species, such as maple, elm, and birch. In spring, after the first burst of growth has stopped and stems have hardened, all leaves are cut off at the base, but the leaf stalk is left so as not to damage the dormant bud in the axil. Within three or four weeks a new set of smaller leaves appears. Leaves are trimmed two or even three times in a growing season. With each successive trimming, dormant buds are activated up and down the branches, and the new sets of leaves soon produce a mass of dense smaller foliage and the beginnings of new proliferated twigs.

Only strong healthy bonsai can be leaf-trimmed, and then only after a full month of fertilizing. Constant trimming is a considerable strain on the stamina of a tree and it may kill a less vigorous specimen. Healthy trees can be leaf-trimmed from the end of May through June and July in northeastern America. Then the leaves that form are half the normal size, or even smaller, and fall coloring is usually much more brilliant.

The first stage of plant growth involves a rapid expansion of vegetative shoots. This is the reason spring growth is vigorous. The internodal spaces are generous and there is less leaf surface. The supply of nitrogen in the buds is at a high level in relation to the supply of carbohydrates, so rapid increase in size takes place.

As the weather becomes warmer the plant has an increased need for water (to support more foliage) and nitrogen until a stage is reached where growth slows down due to shortages of these necessities. Because of these facts, spring is the best time to allow your bonsai to grow to fill out its overall composition and to expand in diameter. However, pruning is a practice that cannot be neglected at this time or the bonsai rapidly grows out of shape.

Many plants pass into a second growth period in late summer or early fall as the supply of carbohydrates increases in proportion to the available nitrogen, but that growth is less vigorous and little pruning is needed to maintain the overall shape. Avoid late summer or early fall pruning, since it may encourage new growth. If you need to prune, wait until the leaves drop and then prune to retain the shape.

PEST CONTROL

Bonsai are susceptible to the same pests that attack their larger relatives; but luckily, because of their miniature size, trouble shows up almost immediately, and prompt remedial measures can be taken. Aphids are the worst pest; they damage leaves and the growing tips of shoots. A mild spray of Malathion mixed

104. For pest control, from left to right: Polyspray recepticle and pump (center) for sprays; a granular systemic insecticide that is sprinkled on top of the soil, where it is dissolved by watering, absorbed by the roots, and carried to branches and leaves; an aerosol spray for control of aphids, which should be held well away from leaves because the repellent will damage them; Malathion is used with Benomyl every two or three weeks as a preventive spray; Bonide systemic granules can be used on most flowering and fruiting trees; Bonide liquid spray; Benomyl, a fungicide, is used as preventive control.

with soapy water usually kills them. Since aphids are often carried to bonsai by ants, spraying table legs with a proper insecticide is a good precaution. Other pests—mealy bugs, scale, rosebugs, Japanese beetles, among many others—may attack bonsai; but with insecticides judiciously used, say, on a monthly basis, control is easy. What is essential is to keep a constant lookout for trouble and then to take prompt remedial action. I have found that preventing pests is better than trying to eradicate them after they are found on your bonsai, so I spray my bonsai once a month with a dilute solution of Malathion and Benomyl. This is a combination of an insecticide, a miticide, and a fungicide.

WINTER CARE

Proper care in winter varies with your home situation and plant-hardiness zone (see appendix D). Contrary to common belief, winter cold as such does not harm bonsai. The damage occurs when freezing dehydrates the plants. With

105. The interior of the cold frame shown in Figure 92. The floor is gravel, which permits drainage and keeps the cold frame moist. Cold frames should be built with a northern exposure to avoid excessive sunlight on bright winter days.

evergreens, there is also the danger of dry, cold winds drawing too much moisture from the needles. If the moisture is not replaced, a tree suffers; and where the ground is frozen it is not possible to give plants water.

There are several solutions for winter care: in cold regions one can use deep cold frames, enclosed porches, garages, cool basements, or plastic or fiberglass cold houses. Each person must make his or her own decision as to the best solution for winter care depending upon the area of the country in which he or she lives.

In hardiness zone 6 I have found that two types of winter care work best: a cold frame and a fiberglass cold-storage house (Figs. 91 and 92). The moisture-loving bonsai are placed in the cold frame in November or early December and left there for the rest of the winter. Usually, weather is mild enough by the first of March to move them out into the open. On warm winter days, when temperatures go above 40°F (about 4.5°C), the cold frame is opened partly, to keep the inside temperature from reaching 60°–70°F (roughly 15.5°–21°C). Such heat is likely to force trees into growth and thus make them liable to winter kill.

Bonsai in a cold frame should be checked twice a month to be sure they are not drying out. Snow may be placed on top of the containers inside the cold frame. The snow, melting as the winter wanes, adds moisture to the soil. Or the bonsai can be watered with a sprinkling can. This is dangerous, however, unless the day is mild, because freezing water may crack the containers.

The bonsai that need drier conditions are placed on benches in the fiberglass cold-storage house at the same time that the others are placed in the cold frame. These bonsai also are moved back outside by the first of March. The fiberglass storage house has extra framing inside so that black plastic can be draped from ceiling to floor to block out sunlight and to create an air layer next to the wall to help protect the plants from the sudden fluctuations of the freeze-thaw cycle. During very cold weather the soils do freeze but the freeze-thaw cycle is a very slow process and does not create a problem. This cold-storage house has a thermostatically controlled fan that draws cold air in when the temperature inside goes above 55°F (about 12.8°C), as is possible during a bright, sunny day. This circulation of air is beneficial for the bonsai but also requires that they be checked for dryness. In the winter they are watered approximately once every two or three weeks when the weather moderates. If we have plenty of snow, the snow is spread over the trees and as it melts it gives the plants the needed moisture.

If you have only a few bonsai and there is space in your garden, you can remove bonsai from containers and set them in the ground for the winter. Select a spot protected from wind and carefully fill soil in around them and tamp it well to avoid air pockets, which might accumulate moisture. Moisture, with alternate freezing and thawing, damages the rootlets. Mulch the soil well up the trunk, and leave the tree until spring. In some places, mice and rabbits can be dangerous, for they may chew bark and twigs in severe winters. A fence of fine chicken wire around bonsai keeps out the marauders.

Bonsai can also be successfully wintered in a cool greenhouse or cold sun room, if there is some protection against rising heat on sunny days. Warmth causes sap to rise and promotes premature growth, which is damaged when the temperature plunges down again.

In every area there are many variations on winter care. You have to assess your own situation and discover the best method. Local nurserymen may be able to advise you, but only if they have some knowledge of bonsai. The best information comes from successful bonsai growers in the same area. Bonsai are not plants that can be neglected at any time of the year.

5. CREATING A
GOOD SOIL MIXTURE

T HE composition of the soil is an essential factor in the successful culture of bonsai. The various elements, the size of the soil particles, and the proportions of the mixture are all to be considered. The container and its contents represent home for a bonsai, and the conditions must be hospitable if a tree is to thrive. A potting mixture has three functions to fulfill: to allow easy rooting, to allow fast drainage, and to supply nutrition. Each of these items will be explained in detail.

FUNCTIONS OF SOIL

It is the soil that holds most of the moisture for growth and maintenance, the mineral elements for food production, and oxygen for roots, and, finally, acts as an anchor for the plant. Through years of experience, Japanese bonsai specialists have accumulated considerable knowledge about the soil requirements of potted trees. Traditionally, the Japanese specialists recommend mixtures of clay, various potting soils, and sand combined in proportions to give each tree conditions comparable to those of its native habitat. However, the rationale for exacting soil formulas is never given in any book on growing bonsai. Few authors seem to agree on soil mixtures, and what works for one person may not automatically work for another. There are so many variable factors in bonsai soil-requirements and personal watering schedules that it is impossible to recommend one soil formula that is better than another. Hence it seems necessary to point out a few facts about soils and their functions and let each person develop his own formulas to meet his own situation.

One factor that is agreed upon by all bonsai growers is the need for excellent drainage. Very few plants can survive long if their roots are kept constantly wet. The reason is that during the processes of photosynthesis and transpiration the leaves and roots of a plant absorb certain substances, such as carbon dioxide and oxygen; and if the soil is constantly wet, the roots cannot carry out their life processes and the plant literally drowns.

SIFTING SOILS

Many of the Japanese books on bonsai recommend sifting the soil and placing it in layers in the container, with the coarsest granules on the bottom and the finest on the top. This sifting and layering of the soil provides three things: excellent drainage, water retention to give moisture when needed, and pore space between the soil particles to allow for an exchange of water and gases. When water is applied to the soil, it soaks in and fills the pore spaces; and as a result, the gases, being lighter than water, are pushed out. If proper drainage exists, the excess water soon drains to a lower level and out the drain hole, allowing gases to be drawn back into the pore spaces as the water leaves. This constant exchange back and forth provides a good environment for the growth and development of a healthy root system. Root tips are very sensitive to gases in the soil, and most of the fine absorbing hairs on a root die if water stands in the root area during the active growth period.

Water in the soil is affected by three forces. One is gravity, which works to pull water downward. The second is adhesion, which tends to hold a thin film of water around each soil particle; and the third is cohesion, which, along with adhesion, resists gravity and causes water to rise by capillary attraction through the narrow passages between soil particles.

Fine soils hold more water than coarse soils for two reasons: they have a greater total surface for water to adhere to and, therefore, have a stronger capillary attraction. These forces together exert more force to retain water than gravity does to move it downward. Therefore, because of the strong action of adhesion and capillary attraction, gravity cannot pull water from a layer of fine soil that is merely moist. But when the soil is completely saturated these forces

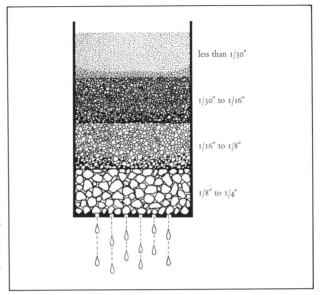

less than 1/30"

1/30" to 1/16"

1/16" to 1/8"

1/8" to 1/4"

106. Soil screened into various sizes and put into a container in layers has a greater capacity to hold both air and water than does uniformly blended soil.

are less effective, and gravity moves the excess water into the soil layers below.

The film of water adhering to or surrounding a soil particle is thicker at the bottom than at the top because of gravity. When particles of soil are stacked on top of one another, the extra thickness of water transfers to the soil particles underneath and so on down in chain fashion. However, when a given droplet of water reaches the bottom of a container, it is supported and the chain effect of gravity is broken.

Where soil is stratified with the largest particles on the bottom, graduating to the smallest size on top, more than twice as much water is retained in comparison with uniformly blended soil particles of mixed sizes. Several factors contribute to this phenomenon. First is that in a regular soil mixture the small particles occupy the spaces between the large particles and thus reduce the volume of pore space available to be occupied by water. Second, in stratified soil there is a phenomenon that occurs at the interface of any two soil layers: water moves with difficulty across the interface. The smaller particles in the upper layer have smaller spaces between them and, therefore, have a strong capillary attraction. Under these circumstances each soil layer must become and remain saturated before water will move into the next layer. Eventually, even the large-particled layer becomes saturated.

What effect does this have on bonsai? Most notable is that in a graded and layered soil there is much more open pore space, which when not filled with water is filled with air. Air is necessary for healthy roots.

107, 108. These screens, made with the lightweight Homosote, are 12" square and 2" deep. When used, they are nested (above left), with the largest screen at the top and the smallest at the bottom. When shaken, soil placed in the top screen will sift through all four screens, leaving three basic grades of soil for potting. From left to right (above right), the screens are one-half-, one-quarter-, one-eighth-, and one-sixteenth-inch mesh; and the resulting soils are (from left to right) bottom soil, main soil, and top soil. Any dust that sifts through the finest screen is discarded and *never* included in a potting medium.

But in addition to ample air, we also get a bonus of extra water because each layer of soil has a greater capacity for retaining water than does mixed-particle blended soil. Because of the large size of bonsai plants in proportion to their pots, this extra capacity to hold water is essential; and complete saturation is not a problem for short periods of time because of the proportionally large losses of water through transpiration. Hence, healthy roots can have both air and water at various depths.

The sifting of soils and the layers of soil provide ample air to the roots, extra water to compensate for large transpirational loss, and a favorable soil climate that makes it easier for plants to absorb nutrients and grow.

Japanese growers use screens of many sizes to sift their soils. Over the years I have found that just four sizes provide the three necessary grades of potting soil. My American-made set of screens is nested so that I can screen all three grades at once (Figs. 107, 108). The screens are of one-half-, one-quarter-, one-eighth-, and one-sixteenth-inch mesh. They are stacked one atop another in sequence, with the smallest mesh on the bottom. Whenever I screen or sift my soils, I place the soil mixture in the top screen, a shovelful at a time. Then I shake the screens back and forth until the soil has sifted through all four screens. The three grades of soil thus obtained are stored separately in twenty-five-gallon plastic cans. The silt that falls through the smallest screen is discarded and *never included* in potting mediums. Soil is always stored in a dry place and mixed as needed for each bonsai when it is repotted in the spring.

From sad experience, I can vouch for the value of sifting. When I started with bonsai, I did not screen soils carefully; and I lost trees that proved, on autopsy, to have rotted roots, the result of too-long-retained moisture. Once I began to sift with care, I lost no more trees from this cause.

Soil Formula

After many years of experimentation I have found a soil formula that is successful for me; it is composed of a basic mixture of approximately one-third each of the following ingredients: fired clay (such as Terra-Green), equal amounts of perlite and Waylite (a material used in lightweight building blocks), and peat moss, with some nutritive substances added in small quantities for certain tree species.

These ingredients are first mixed together and then sifted for use during the potting season. Many different soil ingredients are available throughout the country, but each item has its value in the soil formula.

Importance of Clay

Clay particles are the primary component in potting mediums. In most areas, subsoil dug from about three feet down and dried will yield hard clay pellets. These may be dried, graded, and stored until needed. However, digging this material is difficult and time-consuming; and often the clay is not of the volcanic type, which the Japanese have found best for bonsai, and does not hold together after repeated watering. The clay dissolves into silt and clogs the pore spaces. Terra-Green and Turf-Face are clay products that are mined and fired before being sold and do not break down even after repeated use in a soil mixture. These substances hold one and a half times their own weight in water and act as reservoirs when water is needed.

Perlite, Waylite, Sand, and Drainage

Perlite is a product used by commercial growers to provide aeration and pore space in a potting mixture. If you use it, purchase the coarse horticultural variety, which is available at most garden centers.

Waylite (boiled slag) is a byproduct of iron smelting and is used to make lightweight building blocks for the construction industry. This material is lightweight and porous, like volcanic ash, and it promotes excellent drainage. It can be purchased by the bag wherever Waylite blocks are manufactured.

Sand can be used for drainage; however, it must not be the salty seashore type, which is heavy when wet and adds to the weight of the containers. Salty sand is to be avoided; use builder's sand.

All the above materials encourage the branching of roots and promote drainage. As a rootlet strikes a grain of sand, it turns in another direction, and in a short time a fine network of feeder roots results. Without such roots, twigginess and dense leafing do not develop, since the two systems, the one above ground and the other below, support and promote each other.

Peat, Top Soil, and Humus

Peat is an organic material that is added to soil for the broad-leaved bonsai to give more bulk for feeder roots, to hold more moisture, and to provide an acid medium. Certain bonsai, such as flowering and fruiting trees and the broad-leaved evergreens, are heavy feeders and need additional nutritive materials.

Top soil from a well-worked garden usually contains the humus necessary for healthy bonsai. The soil is spread out in the sun to dry and then sifted through screens of various sizes, as described earlier. I then discard the powdery, silty residue and use only the pellets remaining in the screens. Since time is a factor that is important to me, I have found that it is easier and less time-consuming to buy top soil or humus from a garden shop for use in my potting mixture. Also, the materials are already sterilized and need only to be dried and screened to be ready for use. For most fruiting and flowering trees and broad-leaved evergreens my basic soil formula is used with humus or humus-laden top soil added to the main soil just before potting up these trees. At least twenty-five percent top soil by volume is added to the basic mixture, as these trees are indeed heavy feeders.

Many people growing bonsai pay little attention to the pH requirements of most plants. Such people find that some plants do not grow and thrive as they should, especially western plants that are brought to the east, where the rain is more acid, which does affect plants with a neutral or alkaline pH requirement.

pH Requirements

The pH mentioned above deserves much more attention, for it is a factor that plays a vital role in making nutrients available to plants. In chemistry, pH is a measure of the degree of acidity or alkalinity of a substance, and the pH values of soils affect the growth of bonsai. The pH values are measured on a scale from 1 to 14, where 7 is the center, or neutral point. As readings go down the scale from 7, tested soils contain increasing concentrations of hydrogen ions, which make the reaction acid; above 7, an increasing number of hydroxyl ions make the soil alkaline. Because of the high amount of rainfall in eastern North America, soils automatically become more acid; in the drier parts of the West, the opposite is true—an alkaline condition sets in. The rainfall factor becomes a problem when trying to grow as bonsai specific plant families that have a narrow range of tolerance in their soil pH requirement.

Briefly, the pH requirements of natural vegetation are as follows.

pH less than 3.7: heath or bog thickets
pH 3.7–4.5: tamarack, black spruce, hemlock, aspen, birch
pH 4.5–5.5: the majority of conifers
pH 5.5–6.9: the bulk of deciduous forests
pH 6.9–8.0: neutral to alkaline grasslands

All plants have a pH tolerance within which they will still survive: for instance, the optimum pH range for the genus *Malus* (the apple) is 5.5–6.5. However, they have been found growing in soil that tests as low, or acidic, as 4.0 and as high, or alkaline, as 8.0. Due to an increase in popularity of bonsai, many growers are now advertising and shipping their plants all over the United States. It becomes important to understand the pH requirement of each plant and how this translates into soil usage, if the plants are to survive. In order to keep the soil pH more on the neutral to alkaline side, each time after I fertilize certain plants, I sprinkle a teaspoonful or more of granular limestone upon the surface of the soil in the container so the limestone will dissolve into the soil with subsequent waterings. Trees that need this additional material are junipers, the western pines, and the *Malus* genus.

Mycorrhizae

The term mycorrhiza designates the symbiotic relationship of certain fungi and the roots of certain plants. In the case of pines and related conifers, the hyphae of the fungi penetrate the root tissue and cause a hypertrophied growth similar to the bacterial nodules on legumes. The mycorrhizal association fills several important functions; the extensions of fungi mycelia from a plant's roots are a great benefit to the host tree, increasing as they do the absorbing surface of the roots. Moreover, the mycelia help break down the soil and help make nutrients available to the host plant. A further advantage is that the fungus produces acids that dissolve silicates in soil and is able to absorb released ions and transmit them directly to the main conducting system of the tree.

Mycorrhizae appear as white mold growing among the roots of pines. This mold improves a tree's ability to absorb nutrients and should be present if the tree is to be healthy. The mold can be saved and used in the soil mixture for new trees that do not have the mycorrhizae in their root system. Mycorrhizae are seen with many conifers, such as pine, fir, cedar, juniper, spruce, hemlock, larch, and bald cypress. They can also be found in a few deciduous species, such as birch, hornbeam, beech, and oak.

Timing and Other Soil Considerations

In reviewing the literature, we find a general agreement that conifers should be repotted every three to five years and young plants every year or two. When in training as bonsai, deciduous trees should be repotted every one or two years, with the exception, perhaps, of willow, which is repotted twice a year, since it grows so quickly.

The soil mixture should contain larger and rougher particles for rugged-looking trees and finer particles for trees that are delicate in nature.[4] With deciduous trees, most of the soil around the roots can be removed when repotting. However, with conifers, only part of the soil around the roots is removed: in several areas around the perimeter of the soil ball, pie-shaped wedges of old soil can be combed out and new soil filled in in these areas to keep the trees producing new fine roots.

4. Naka, *Bonsai Techniques*, p. 114.

6. BONSAI MATERIAL FROM THE WILD OR THE NURSERY

BONSAI can be created from almost any perennial plant material, but certain semiwoody or woody species are preferable because of their genetic makeup and habits of growth. Many native American species have fine branching patterns and small needles or leaves, so that a bonsai developed from them will have all parts in proportion in miniature. Such wild stock is excellent for bonsai and is as good as, or even better than, the Japanese species traditionally selected for bonsai. For example, there is the eastern red cedar, a small-needled, shaggy-barked, easily-trained species that takes readily to pot culture because of its fibrous root system. It has as many virtues for bonsai as any evergreen. Although it is a common wilding over perhaps a third of the United States, it is difficult to locate in nurseries.

I am partial to indigenous plants because, more than any others, they can communicate a sense of locale. The suggestion is subtle, but the development of native material seems to me to make the difference between fine original American bonsai and simple reinterpretation of the Japanese forms.

Local varieties, especially the understory trees and shrubs (those plants that grow under larger plants) from the edges of woodlands, are too often ignored. Yet they have outstanding possibilities as bonsai. Americans have the small-needled red cedar, the small-leaved hornbeam, and many varieties with charming flowers, such as the serviceberry, the spicebush, and the nannyberry. The winterberry, when free of leaves, is still bright, with its scarlet berries; the maleberry, a relative of the huckleberry, holds clusters of gray-green fruits throughout the year. The deciduous trees of northeastern America are the glory of autumn, with the colorful brilliant red foliage of maples, the canary yellow of birches, and the maroon of blueberry shrubs that hug the ground. And these are only a very few of the native treasures well suited to bonsai.

Naturally dwarfed plants are prized in Japan and were probably the source of the original bonsai. In most countries where appropriate conditions exist there is an unlimited number of natural dwarfs, if you have the patience to search for them. When you collect, however, be mindful of proprietary rights and laws; and always secure permission from the owner or the state before scouting fields and woods to dig up specimens. On abandoned farm land, I have located fine specimens of apple, eastern red cedar, hornbeam, pitch pine, winterberry, beech, willow, blueberry, laurel, hemlock, black birch, and bittersweet. The soil that drove the farmer out produces a wealth of ideal bonsai material. Indeed each ecological area offers many typical species, and the list could include a great many more plants.

Not all natural dwarfs are suitable for bonsai; stunted growth alone will not make a good bonsai. The basic form of the plant is the determining factor. When you spot a possible bonsai candidate, try to visualize the final composition and estimate what you can accomplish with patient training. If a tree does not have inherent possibilities for a bonsai, do not bother with it.

In *Bonsai Techniques,* John Naka points out that there are five basic elements that one should look for in selecting plant material for bonsai.

1. ROOTS   The roots should spread in all directions from the base of the trunk.
2. TRUNK   The trunk should taper as it ascends to the top of the tree.
3. APEX   Every tree should have a top or apex.
4. PRIMARY BRANCHES   Primary branches should be thick and full in the lower portions of the tree and become smaller and thinner toward the top of the tree.
5. SECONDARY BRANCHES   The secondary branches should have plenty of foliage.

These five basic elements in selecting bonsai material apply to both wild and nursery material. Many plants do not have the basic characteristics to make good bonsai and there is little the amateur can do to improve them. So do not waste time; select with care.

The best time to look for material in colder areas is in the winter, after the leaves have fallen and you can see through the brush. Then you can clearly observe the shape of the trunk and can assess the quality of a design. If the ground is not yet frozen, you can also scratch away the soil to see whether any large surface roots exist. A tree that seems worthwhile can be marked with a piece of string or cloth to make it easy to find in the spring. It also helps to record the location and type of material in a notebook.

The best time to collect is in the spring, when swelling buds indicate the end of dormancy. The actual date varies with local conditions and also with the species. Some species bud out much earlier than others.

Because of the great differences in the time that spring arrives in various parts of North America, it is wise to consult an agricultural-zone map to determine when the last hard frost is likely to occur. You can safely dig plants at that time. However, as the buds swell and the plant puts out long new shoots, it can be risky to collect and it might be better to wait until fall or the following spring; although I do know bonsai growers who collect plants as early as December in Texas and California, since spring comes early in those parts of the country and they do not generally experience hard winters.

In desert regions some plants can be collected in the hottest summer months, since the severe heat causes them to become dormant or semidormant. If you collect in the mountains, remember: the higher the elevation the later spring will occur.

Usually a wild specimen has a poor root system and should be root-pruned *in place* for several years before it is removed. This pruning will induce new and finer root development. A good method is to prune in place one-half of the old roots the first year. With a sharp spade, dig a six- to eight-inch-deep trench halfway round the plant at the drip line: then fill in the trench with fresh soil rich in humus. This will encourage fine feeder roots to grow out. The next year similarly prune the other side of the root system. If necessary, repeat the procedure the following year, although a tree can usually be dug up by the third year.

Root-pruning in place is by far the safest way to handle a plant, and it is the only way that a tree with a large tap root or an extended root system can be removed and still live. However, this method is not always practical, particularly when the tree is far away from your home. If a tree is healthy and it is possible to remove it with a good-sized ball of roots and soil, you can dig at once and take a chance that it will survive. A tree with all its foliage should be dug at least as far from the trunk as the drip line, although a dormant deciduous tree can be removed with somewhat less soil. Evergreens, however, should always be dug up with as much root system and soil as possible. With any tree, dig with care and avoid cutting large roots close to the trunk. Keep the root ball moist by covering it with burlap or plastic, and plant the tree in a garden as soon as possible. There you can give it special attention for a year or two, until that important fine network of fibrous roots develops.

If the tree has a poor root system or roots too large to cut safely, give it up, unless bulldozers threaten and the tree is destined to die anyway. Some specimens, though attractive, are simply not for collecting.

Natural Bonsai from Collected Malus

With the expansion of railroads in the nineteenth century, many New York and New England farmers departed for the fertile midwestern prairie lands; others moved into the expanding cities. In time their cultivated fields returned to woodland. Seedlings shot up in abandoned orchards and grew unattended for years, naturally dwarfed and excellent for bonsai. Some of my bonsai were located growing under just such conditions in northwestern Connecticut and the central Hudson Valley in New York. They started as seedlings but never reached tree size, since they were browsed by cattle and deer. Those trees were perfect specimens for bonsai. The trunks were short and thick, and the shapes were most fascinating, with twisting branches and a fine ramification of twigs.

In the spring of 1958, from an abandoned orchard I dug three apple trees to be developed into bonsai. Their long anchor roots were pruned, and each tree was planted in half of an old nail keg. Where necessary to improve the basic shape, some of the long branches were removed, and all remaining branches were cut back to within eight inches of the main trunk. The pruning of the branches was necessary in order to reduce each tree to a size that would be in scale with its overall composition.

Each year the new shoots were allowed to grow long, until fall, to achieve thickness. In the spring the branches were cut back to improve the design, or were eliminated if not needed. This process was repeated for three years to give the bonsai a branch structure that could be shaped by wiring. During the fourth year the branches were allowed to grow long from spring until the middle of June, when the green growth was woody enough for the branches to be wired into their basic design. Over a period of about eighteen years there has been a minimum of wiring; however, with much pruning of shoots, these trees have developed into bonsai of distinctive and artistic shapes.

The first styling and shaping with copper wire brought into focus the major shape and character of each bonsai. Several times during the eighteen years I had black-and-white photographs taken of each tree and had several prints made of each tree so that I could cut up a print. The outline of an individual tree was cut out and pasted on illustration board; with a pencil I would sketch in the details of how I thought the tree would look in the future. That exercise helped me to look at tree shapes and design elements in other bonsai.

The *Malus* bonsai I collected in 1958 are kept on my bonsai bench in full sun from the middle of March to the end of November. During the winter months they are housed in a large fiberglass cold-storage house, protected from wind and winter sun, just as described in the section on winter care in chapter 4.

The trees begin bud initiation in late February or early March as they become active again after dormancy. If the trees are left in the fiberglass house too long, their first leaves may appear. At that stage, it is important to get the trees outside to cool off in order to delay the growing process until weather conditions become more stable and repotting, if necessary, is safe. In my part of America, New Jersey, one can sometimes begin repotting as early as April fifteenth. The need for vigilance when trees come out of their dormancy was an important lesson I had to learn about winter care and spring repotting; and it was a sad one, since I learned it through the death of some delightful specimens.

Removing trees from the protection of a storage house or cold frame returns them to a state of dormancy: they should not be root-pruned until they become active again, when the weather begins to warm up. Take your cue from the indigenous trees in the ground around your growing area before you attempt repotting.

Trees of the *Malus* genus are not fussy about their soil requirements; however, the soil should be neither too rich nor too poor. If excess food is available, the trees produce an exorbitant mass of branches and leaves at the expense of flowers. If the soil is completely worn out, the plants will have to struggle for survival and will not become healthy specimens.

During the growing season, *Malus* are fertilized once a week with a water-

109. A common apple collected in the spring of 1958. Photographed in September, 1963. After cutting the branches back, new shoots were allowed to grow.

110. The back of the tree, photographed in September, 1963.

soluble fertilizer that is low in nitrogen. In my area the growing season starts in mid–April and extends through the end of August. All fertilizing is ceased at the end of August to allow the new wood to harden before frosts begin in late September or early October. The trees should be given full sunlight so they will make enough food to produce flower buds the following year. Some trees seem reluctant to generate flower buds for years. However, if the trees are healthy, I reduce their nitrogen intake and feed them potassium and phosphorus to induce flowering. In order to keep the pH value between 5.5 and 6.5 for my *Malus,* I place two teaspoonfuls of powdered limestone around the edges of the containers three or four times during the growing season.

The *Malus* genus is susceptible to many types of diseases and insect damage. When collected, my trees were filled with borer and oystershell scale. At the beginning of the first growing season after uprooting, each tree was sprayed with a dormant oil spray containing an insecticide, a miticide, and a fungicide to give the trees the protection they needed. Currently I am using a commercial product marketed by Bonide Chemical Co. under the trade name Bonide. This all-purpose spray compound seems to give the trees adequate protection from all diseases and pests.

111. The tree in November, 1967. It has begun to assume the shape of its ultimate design.

112. Detail of the back of the tree, showing scars from pruning and removing branches to effect the overall design. Photographed in February, 1968.

The photographs in Figures 109–15 were taken over a period of thirteen years, after the subject trees had been removed from the nail kegs and training had been initiated. The original cutting back and selection of the front were accomplished under the direction of Yuji Yoshimura. For the past several years, the refinement process has consisted simply of pruning and a minimum of wiring.

During the summer of 1975, Kyūzō Murata and Masakuni Kawasumi visited the area where I live and were shown the apple tree in the photographs. Both gentlemen seemed to enjoy this American bonsai, and when requested to offer critical comments, both immediately turned it around to view it from the back. Also, each commented that it needed a larger container. The photographs show the tree from both the front and the back; Figures 114 and 115 show its old and new front in a larger container.

The tree has been repotted in a new container, a new front has been established, and the bonsai will be pruned to continue its refinement into a mature bonsai. This is the evolution of a natural bonsai collected from an old apple orchard. The apple is such an adaptable plant that it deserves to be found in every bonsai collection.[5]

5. American Bonsai Society, *Bonsai Journal* 10, no. 3 (fall, 1976), p. 51.

I trained my first collected apple to an informal upright style, utilizing the natural pattern of the trunk, although in the field the tree grew almost straight up and down. As I fashioned it into a bonsai, I removed one major branch and urged a secondary branch with a finely tapered terminal to extend the line of the trunk. The main branches were wired into more nearly horizontal positions to force new buds and initiate the development of a fine network of twigs. The branches were arranged around the trunk in groups of three, the first branch to the right, the second to the left, and the third to the rear of the tree. The first third of the trunk was left exposed. As dormant buds broke through the bark, I pinched them off before they could grow out and destroy the clean line of the trunk.

Another specimen, shown in Figures 116–19, was also developed eighteen years ago by drastic pruning and wiring and potting in a large Japanese mirror-style container. The tree had a handsome, naturally twisted trunk, but it was too tall and had to be shortened. When I cut off the greater part of two major branches, a potentially ugly Y formation appeared, so I planted the tree at an angle in the container. This effectively minimized the Y and at the same time accentuated the tree's graceful line. In subsequent seasons the branches have been further pruned and wired to enhance the basic shape.

113. Photographed in January, 1967, the tree shows more detail in branch structure and twig network.

114. The bonsai set in a larger container, as suggested by Mr. Kyūzō Murata.

115. The bonsai turned around, displaying the new front.

When these trees were collected, they were infested with borers, which had made large holes in the trunks and main branches (Figs. 120, 121), a not unusual condition with wild *Malus* specimens. The borers were eliminated by injecting Borerkil into the holes, which were then sealed over with plastic clay and later with cement (Fig. 122). The ends of all trimmed branches were treated with a tree-healing paint to prevent disease.

Scale was also present and I controlled it with a dormant oil spray. With wild stock such attention is almost always necessary: the poor conditions that produce desirable specimens also make them weak and susceptible to trouble. My apple trees have responded to good culture and are now healthy and producing vigorous new growth each year. Collected trees, well cared for, develop into excellent bonsai over a period of time.

Although natural dwarfs are to be found in every part of America, good bonsai material cannot be located on every expedition. I rarely come home empty-handed, however; I always find some ferns, grasses, wildflowers, or mosses that are not covered by conservation laws, which, of course, must be respected wherever you collect. I am always on the lookout for seedlings of native trees that, despite their attractiveness as shade trees and ornamentals, are less readily available in nurseries than trees of Asian or European origin.

116. Taken in 1963, six years after the tree was collected, this photograph shows the basic Y formation of the main branches. Notice where the tops of the branches were pruned back to form new terminals.

117. This photograph taken in 1976 shows how the main branch has begun to thicken and a new apex has developed.

SOME FINE NATIVE PLANTS FOR BONSAI

AMERICAN BEECH, *Fagus grandifolia*   This tall forest tree, which has a smooth, steel-gray bark and a golden fall foliage that turns a papery brown and hangs on all winter, makes a handsome bonsai. Its large leaves reduce in size under good bonsai culture.

BITTERSWEET, *Celastrus scandens*   This woody vine can be trained in various ways. It has large leaves and beautiful red-orange berries that hold in autumn after the leaves fall.

BLUEBERRY, *Vaccinium* spp.   These shrubs of fields and barren lands have many forms and are frequently dwarfed. They have small leaves, tiny white or pinkish flowers, bluish fruits, and spectacular maroon and purple fall coloring.

118. This photograph of the back of the tree, taken in the spring of 1977, shows the growth of the main branch and apex.

119. The tree in fruit in June, 1977.

EASTERN RED CEDAR, *Juniperus virginiana*   This common evergreen, with small needles, fibrous roots, and an interesting shaggy bark, is ideal for bonsai culture.

EASTERN HEMLOCK, *Tsuga canadensis*   This small-needled evergreen is common in shaded, damp forests; dwarf sports occur. A closely related species, the western hemlock, *T. heterophylla,* is found west of the Rocky Mountains.

AMERICAN HORNBEAM, *Carpinus caroliniana*   This understory tree is found in eastern hardwood forests. Its leaves reduce in size when it is container grown. An easily propagated tree, it is valuable for its brilliant red fall coloring.

MOUNTAIN LAUREL, *Kalmia latifolia*   This broad-needled evergreen shrub has pinkish-white spring flowers of extraordinary beauty, a naturally graceful form, and a furrowed bark. The sheep laurel, *Kalmia angustifolia,* a related species with reddish flowers, is smaller in all respects.

120. The main trunk of a collected apple showing borer damage. The area was cleaned out, and lime sulfur was applied to protect the wood.

121. The borer hole extends down into and through the trunk (white backing has been used to make the hole clearly visible).

PITCH PINE, *Pinus rigida* This pine, common along sandy barrens, seashores, and glacial lake beds, is very hardy and just as easy to train as the Japanese black pine. The pitch pine is furthermore desirable because it sends out buds from mature bark and its needles will become shorter under culture.

WINTERBERRY, OR BLACK ALDER, *Ilex verticillata* This is an understory tree of wet locations. Deciduous, with bright red berries that appear along its twigs in autumn, it is very like the deciduous Japanese holly, *Ilex serrata,* although it is smaller in every respect.

NURSERY MATERIAL

Collecting plants from the wild will not tempt all bonsai enthusiasts. Some may not care to scout the fields and woods; others will not find it convenient. Perhaps collecting native plants is a hobby within a hobby. Nursery stock is available to everyone and most American bonsai are started from nursery plants. Even the ardent collector of native material usually gets half his stock from nurseries.

There is no question that nursery browsing is easier, less demanding, and more

122. The trunk was filled with cement, coated with wood dough, and painted with lime sulfur to prevent the trunk from snapping off if the tree is blown off the bench.

123. This collected wisteria has been treated in the same manner to preserve its trunk.

comfortable. The plants may not be so spectacular as some of the dwarfs you find in the wild, but they can still be rewarding. Each of us develops his own routine for combing the nursery rows; we learn how to judge potential material and we try not to rush our decisions. Perhaps the best place to start is the discard corner, where nurserymen relegate plants unsuitable for landscape work. Frequently, these plants have dwarfed trunks, twisted forms, or irregular branching —all valuable characteristics of bonsai stock.

SEEDLINGS AND CUT-DOWN STOCK

There are two types of material to be searched for. First are the seedlings that you can nurture, prune, train, and generally develop, over a period of many years, into attractive bonsai. If possible, put the seedlings directly into the ground, where they can be worked on easily. Each year fertilize, trim, leaf-trim, and root-prune them. With this treatment, they will develop thicker trunks than if they grew in pots, and the trimming will produce proportionate branching and twigginess.

The other type of nursery material is already mature, with large solid trunks

124. This juniper, *Juniperus squamata wilsonii,* was developed from nursery stock. Photograph taken in 1966.

125. The same tree in 1977, when it had been in training for eighteen years.

and main branches. Height is not important, since the upper parts can be radically pruned back to the desired size. We call this "cut-down stock." It can be made into charming instant bonsai if it is potted up at the beginning of spring and trained over the growing season to refine the shape and fill in the cut away areas.

Be careful in your selection of plants to be cut down, or the results may be regrettable. Usually there are many plants to choose from. The trunk line and the position of the heavy branches are the determining factors. Examine a tree carefully to make sure you can cut away unwanted parts and still have a fundamentally pleasing form. If possible, examine the root system to see if it can be used to advantage. Try to visualize the final product from its present state.

Nursery stock is either balled-and-burlapped or canned. The canned plants are excellent for bonsai, since their fully established, fibrous root system makes it possible for training to be started immediately. Furthermore, such plants are already conditioned to a reduced environment, and root- and top-pruning cause minimal shock.

One such can-grown specimen, trained for twenty years, is shown in Figures 124 and 125. I found it at a local nursery, part of a large shipment of prostrate junipers, *Juniperus squamata wilsonii,* a common spreading ornamental with slightly glaucous foliage. Like most junipers, it is excellent for bonsai because of its hardiness, its exfoliating bark, and the long life of its needles. To find it, I searched through the juniper section, tree by tree, finally selecting it for its obvious potential as a cascade. Originally, large branches jutted out from the right side of the trunk, and these were removed entirely, along with many smaller branches on the left side that hid the line of the trunk and the system of cascading branches.

I inserted a heavy wire into the soil at the base of the trunk and wound the wire around the trunk all the way to the end of the longest branch, thus making the branch an extension of the trunk. A second wire was led out of the soil and directed to the forward branch. The manipulation of these two wires produced the initial form. Then with finer wires, I wound the secondary branches, including the three principal limbs at the back. Coaxed into position, these gave depth and width to the tree. Over subsequent growing seasons the wiring has been replaced to accommodate new growth and maintain form. With any juniper a little lime sprinkled over the soil and watered in once or twice a year helps to maintain the lovely subtle color of the needles.

Bonsai from Nursery Plants

COTONEASTER, *Cotoneaster horizontalis, C. apiculata* There are many forms of this plant, which has small leaves, white to pinkish-red flowers, and red-orange fruit.

JAPANESE MAPLE, *Acer palmatum* This is one of the most popular of the deciduous plants and has red or green leaves. Select a deep container, for the leaves have a tendency to burn if the plants are set in shallow pots.

JUNIPER, *Juniperus* spp. Many of the small-needled junipers make good bonsai, especially the green and blue forms and the low, compact, spreading types.

MUGHO PINE, *Pinus mugo* This shrubby tree has small, straight, compact needles. Available in most nurseries, it withstands considerable dryness and requires full sun.

KURUME AZALEA, *Rhododendron obtusum* Varieties of this small-leaved evergreen offer flowers in a wide range of colors and many sizes. Look for specimens with single heavy trunks. Growth sprouts quickly from old wood.

Bonsai with Flowers

Flowering bonsai are grown for the beauty of the display when blossoms are at their peak. Many bloom in spring, a few in summer and autumn. The common flowering bonsai are apricot, azalea, camellia, cherry, crape myrtle, forsythia, gardenia, jasmine, magnolia, sweet olive, peach, pear, plum, quince, rhododendron, winter sweet (or bridal wreath), and wisteria. All are available in American nurseries. If you prefer bonsai that flower you can make a selection that will give you something in bloom throughout the growing season. Some plants can be enjoyed twice, first with flowers and later with fruit. For a succession of bloom, you might select apricot, forsythia, azalea, rhododendron, wisteria, crape myrtle, and camellia or gardenia. These last two bloom both spring and fall.

For cool summer pictures, grow dwarf bamboo, golden willow, nandin, tamarisk, and various grasses. These are frequently displayed with stones laid in basins of sand and water, and they are indeed a refreshing sight on a hot summer day.

BONSAI FOR FALL COLOR AND FRUIT

For brilliant autumn color, American trees are, of course, outstanding. In nurseries you can find barberry, beech, birch, Chinese elm, euonymous, ginkgo, hornbeam, ivy, maple, and oak. These are all handsome in winter after their leaves have fallen and the intricate pattern of twigs becomes visible.

Bonsai with brightly colored fruits are also delightful, although the fruits are rarely in proportion to the trees. Cotoneasters, hawthorns, hollies, and some crab apples will produce small fruits, just as they do in nature. Apples, pomegranates, and citrus species yield fruits of standard size and cannot be induced to bear smaller fruits as bonsai, although we can force them to produce smaller leaves. In Japan, fruiting trees are very popular; in America their charms are just beginning to be appreciated. (For this classification by display value, I am indebted to Lynn R. Perry's *Bonsai: Trees and Shrubs*.)

7. REGIONAL VARIATIONS IN CARING FOR BONSAI

THE continent of North America has such vast regional variations in climate and soil that one species of tree grown in the ground in New York state may be tall, while in Manitoba, Canada, it might be just a bushy shrub. Climate variations alone can cause such differences. From Canada to Texas, the astonishing range of climates, soils, altitudes, and exposure to the elements has an undeniable effect on plant life.

Five identifiable regions in North America differ greatly in their growing conditions (see appendix D). A person interested in bonsai will have to adapt his methods of care to his environment—from the frigid north to desert or humid swampland—and deal imaginatively with its extremes. He will also have to choose knowledgeably those plants that are suited to his local conditions.

"The regional boundaries are only approximate; one merges with the next, and within a general region, the growing conditions will vary to a great extent. The five regions . . . are: the northeast north-central states and adjacent Canada; the seaboard from Florida to Texas; southern California and the desert interior; the Rocky Mountain region; and the Pacific northwest and British Columbia."[6]

Some suggestions for care in each of these regional areas are needed to help the beginner develop his bonsai and understand his region's requirements for growing bonsai. The suggestions offered here include a calendar of work: things

6. Reader's Digest, *Complete Book of the Garden* (Pleasantville, N.Y.: Reader's Digest Association, 1966), p. 585.

to do in the spring, summer, fall, and winter; a schedule for repotting, wiring, and trimming bonsai; some recommendations on fertilizing; and a brief list of plants native to the region that are suitable for bonsai culture.

THE NORTHEAST NORTH-CENTRAL REGION AND ADJACENT CANADA

The great temperate region of Canada and North America stretches approximately eighteen hundred miles from east to west, from the Atlantic coast of Nova Scotia and Maine to the prairies of the Dakotas. From north to south, this region in general experiences a long, cold winter (from November to April); and the growing season is restricted to about five months. Low winter temperatures characterize all the region; but in some areas the weather may vary from the very severe to the more moderate, depending on exposure to wind, the presence of large bodies of water, or the altitude, with more severe conditions occurring at higher elevations.

For the bonsai novice the calendar of work starts in the spring, usually when the bonsai are removed from winter protection, late in March or early in April; although, depending on weather conditions, this can be as late as April 15–30 in some areas. If in doubt about the date in your area, observe the natural trees around you. When they begin to show signs of activity in the spring, your bonsai can safely be removed from winter storage. If bonsai have been stored in cold frames, heated garages, or a greenhouse and they have put out new growth, they will need protection should the temperature drop below freezing, for removing them from protective winter storage returns them to a state of dormancy. They should not be repotted until they show active growth. In this region it is crucial to know when to bring bonsai out of their winter storage.

The basic spring activities in this region are repotting established bonsai if needed, fertilizing those bonsai that are growing, and developing new plants (except conifers) by drastic pruning and shaping with copper wire to set the basic design. It is necessary to inspect certain deciduous trees, such as the beech, hornbeam, maple, hackberry, and the deciduous Japanese holly, which are susceptible to twig damage from the cold, and to prune out any dead wood.

Wiring should be examined during the summer, when the primary growing season has passed, growth has hardened, and the pace of repotting and pruning has slowed down. Inspect wires carefully, since the diameter of new growth may increase more than you have anticipated. The marks resulting from too-tight wires are not only unsightly but hard to cover up: it takes three or four years of new growth for them to disappear, if they ever do.

In June it is important to adjust all bonsai according to sun, shade, and water preferences for the duration of the hot summer months ahead. Wildflowers, accessory plants, and understory plants can be placed under larger bonsai so they do not dry out so fast. Pines and junipers need full sun all day; however, by midsummer they should be turned 180° to ensure they get sun on all sides. All bonsai should be rotated. Certain shade-loving plants should be placed where they receive some shade by about two or three in the afternoon, since the containers absorb heat in the late setting sun, which can cause root damage to certain species, such as deciduous holly and maple.

Spraying bonsai for pests is an activity that continues throughout the growing season in order to prevent damage to the leaves and stems caused by chewing insects. Spraying with a combination of insecticide and fungicide on a monthly basis is the best preventive measure to keep bonsai free of pests and disease.

During the fall bonsai should be prepared for the long hard winter in this region. Fetilizing should stop by the end of August. If the last fertilization is limited to phosphorus and potash, plants will have less dieback, more strength for spring bloom, and better winter resistance.

In order to be properly winter hardened, plants should be left outside through October and November, if the weather allows. This will lessen the chance of twig dieback.

There are several types of winter protection that can be provided for bonsai. You can, for example, sink them (in their pots) into the soil up to the first branch and then cover the soil with a deep mulch to prevent repeated freezing and thawing. The trees can be protected with bamboo-lath shades, screen, or burlap, to prevent sunscald or desiccation. Another type of winter protection is a cold frame, cold house, or storage area, such as a garage or toolhouse, since dormant plants do not require sunlight.

Winter is a season of little activity for bonsai in this region, unless you have a winter-storage area that is accessible so that you can wire and shape pines and prune older wood on deciduous trees. Bonsai should be checked monthly for dryness and watered on mild days, if possible. It is also wise to keep an eye out for signs that mice or other rodents are chewing on the bark. They can destroy a bonsai in just a few days by completely girdling the trunk. Chicken wire will keep rabbits out but traps or some type of rodent poison is necessary to eliminate mice or rats.

Hardy plants found in the northeast north-central region and adjacent Canada that can be used for bonsai include:

paper birch, *Betula papyrifera*
hackberry, *Celtis* spp.
European larch, *Larix decidua*
apple and crab apple, *Malus* spp.
Chinese elm, *Ulmus parvifolia*
cotoneaster, *Cotoneaster* spp.
serviceberry, *Amelanchier* spp.
dwarf winged-bark euonymus, *Euonymus alata compacta*
forsythia, *Forsythia* spp.
spirea, *Spiraea* spp.
spruce, *Picea* spp.
pine, *Pinus* spp.
juniper, *Juniperus* spp.
eastern hemlock, *Tsuga canadensis*
Virginia creeper, *Parthenocissus quinquefolia*
partridgeberry, *Mitchella repens,* as a ground cover

THE SOUTHEAST AND THE GULF REGION

The great coastal plain stretches roughly from Norfolk, Virginia, to Brownsville, Texas, across all or portions of nine states with shores on the Atlantic Ocean or the Gulf of Mexico: Virginia, North Carolina, South Carolina, Georgia, Florida, Alabama, Mississippi, Louisiana, and Texas.

The range of this region is from cool subtropical to warm subtropical. The coastal climate of the southern Atlantic and Gulf states is characterized by high humidity, long, hot summers, and mild winters. Farther inland, beyond the influence of the sea, winters are colder, summers hotter. There are periods when the temperature inland or at high elevations may drop 40°F (about 22.2°C) or more in a very short time, with the lower temperatures accompanied by very dry icy air. Although these cold periods may last only two or three days and nights, such a sudden drop in temperature may injure plants; therefore, some protection is needed for bonsai until the weather is more stable.

The calendar of work for the Southeast and Gulf region includes activity almost year round, since bonsai are simply heeled in during the winter months.

In spring, which comes early to this region (usually late in February or during March), bonsai will be removed from their heeling-in areas, since cold frames, cold greenhouses, or deep pits are rarely used here for winter protection. Most winter-hardy specimens can be heeled in in a raised bed or large box with good drainage, which has been filled with rotted pine sawdust or any other medium that conserves moisture but does not stay too wet. Heeling plants in protects them from drying out.

If you live in a coastal area, it is not even necessary to heel your plants in, so watering is a chore that cannot be neglected. Because of the hot sun in the south, bonsai cannot be allowed to bask, unprotected, in the sun. Natural shade gives adequate protection, or a properly placed hedge can serve the same purpose. If natural protection is not available, then a screen or a shade house can be constructed to filter out the sun's rays and create an agreeable atmosphere for bonsai. In some areas, repotting can be started in late February and during March; however, in the higher elevations inland spring will not arrive until early April. At higher altitudes there will be frost one or two times during this period and some plants may need protection if their growth is tender.

Summer in the south is characterized by intense sun, hot days, and high humidity, which bring problems in controlling pests, as well as certain types of fungus or powdery mildew. To avoid these problems, try to keep trees in a well-ventilated area, where there is plenty of air movement, and where they receive as much sunlight as they can tolerate. Moreover, all plants should be sprayed at weekly intervals with a combination of an insecticide and a fungicide. If possible, water bonsai in the morning and avoid watering from late afternoon to evening.

From June to October, growers in the coastal areas must be prepared for storms of savage intensity, so it becomes important to design a display area near a safe shelter, where bonsai can be protected during a storm should they have to be moved quickly.

During the summer all bonsai should be checked for wires that have become too tight, and pruning should be continued when necessary. Remember to turn your bonsai for strong, healthy twigs and foliage developed evenly on all sides. Certain plants, such as weeping willow, bald cypress, and wisteria, should be kept in a shallow basin of water all summer because they have a need for exorbitant amounts of water.

Activities lessen in the fall, as plant growth slows down; however, wires should be examined, since thickening occurs as food is stored in the roots. In areas where winters are less severe, some bonsai, such as crape myrtle and willow and some of the fruiting bonsai, like crab apple, pear, and cherry, can be repotted in the fall. Some bonsai growers also fertilize in the fall with a fertilizer that is low in nitrogen, since roots are growing and you do not want to stimulate any top growth.

Winter in the higher elevations inland is colder and bonsai need to be heeled in for the winter. Certain bonsai, such as gardenia, crape myrtle, and pomegranate, need some warmth and are kept a little drier. Discontinue top pruning and allow the wood to harden up; your pruning should be done in the spring, when the plants become active again. Those areas near the coast will be having cooler weather and more rain, so it may be necessary to shelter some bonsai, like pine, that need drier conditions. During this period there can be frost, so it is wise to listen carefully to weather reports. Certain plants will need protection against frost and should be brought inside. Quick freezes and subsequent thawing can cause the bark to split on azaleas and gardenias, so limit their watering to morning hours in order to minimize the danger of freezing.

Bonsai materials that are found in the Southeast and Gulf region include:
sugarberry, *Celtis laevigata*
sweet gum, *Liquidambar styraciflua*
redbud, *Cercis canadensis*
crape myrtle, *Lagerstroemia indica*
deodar cedar, *Cedrus deodara*
false cypress, *Chamaecyparis obtusa, C. pisifera,* and *C. thyoides*
eastern red cedar, *Juniperus virginiana*
privet, *Ligustrum* spp.
pine, *Pinus* spp.
live oak, *Quercus virginiana*
mock orange, *Philadelphus coronarius*
spirea, *Spiraea* spp.
camellia, *Camellia japonica* and *C. sasanqua*
myrtle, *Myrtus communis*
podocarpus, *Podocarpus macrophyllus* var. *maké*
ivy, *Hedera* spp.
jasmine, *Jasminum* spp.
Chinese wisteria, *Wisteria sinensis*
star jasmine, *Trachelospermum jasminoides*
bougainvillaea, *Bougainvillaea* spp.
azalea, *Rhododendron* spp.

In frost-free areas the black olive, *Bucida buceras,* and the banyan tree, *Ficus benghalensis,* can be used for bonsai.

The Southwest and Most of California

This region has a climate that ranges from the near tropical to the tropical and even to the alpine. In the Los Angeles area, for instance, tropical bananas and papayas may be growing within sight of snowy mountain valleys where the climate is similar to that of North Dakota.

A narrow strip of land beginning on the Pacific coast and extending to the north and east from San Diego, across the low deserts to Yuma and Phoenix, has mild winters. In this area, free from prolonged winter chilling, some plants fail to become dormant, and some deciduous fruit trees bloom erratically over a long period.

The Southwest may be divided into approximately eight different micro-environments. The bonsai grower should become familiar with his own area and assess the types of plants that can be grown there and the kind of protection they are going to need during the year, depending on the weather.

One area, southward from Morro Bay, California, along the coast to Mexico, seldom has freezing weather. Although the inner coastal regions, such as the San Fernando, San Gabriel, and La Canada valleys, separated from the ocean by mountains, hardly ever have any snow, subtropical plants need protection on cold winter nights.

An area northward from Morro Bay, along the coast to San Francisco and Oakland, has moderate winters and cooler summers, and snow there is rare in winter.

Salinas Valley, the coastal valley north of Morro Bay, and the peninsula south of San Francisco to San Jose are slightly warmer in both winter and summer.

California's great central valley, San Joaquin, has a long growing season, but cool winter temperatures. The valleys farther inland, such as Pomona and San Bernardino, experience great fluctuations in temperatures in summer and winter and plants there need some winter protection.

The desert areas at high elevations (such as Antelope Valley, most of the Mojave Desert, and including areas near Phoenix and south of Tucson) are colder than inner valleys, whereas the desert areas at lower elevations (such as Palm

Springs, Yuma, Phoenix, and the Salt River Valley) have generally high temperatures that moderate somewhat during the winter.

One of the best ways a beginner in any region can obtain reliable information on the care of bonsai under extreme conditions is by talking with more experienced bonsai growers in his area. If this is not feasible, then ask the advice of nearby nurserymen, especially those handling the tender seedlings used for lining-out stock and container-grown plants.

Spring comes early to the Southwest, around the end of February in some areas, so that repotting of certain deciduous material, such as maples and elms, can be started then. It is necessary to have a place where the bonsai can be given protection if there is a sudden dip in the temperature. If necessary to improve their shape, some of the flowering plants, like quince, can be pruned at this time. The pruning of pines and other conifers will have to wait until a little later, when the weather warms up and becomes more stable.

Summers in this region are likely to be hot and dry, so one must make provisions for bonsai to be moved into partial shade during June, July, August, and September. Watering cannot be neglected at any time. If you have small bonsai, for added protection from dryness they can be placed in a tray of moist sand for the duration of the summer. The pots should be buried almost up to the rim. Check the containers every three or four weeks and examine the roots. If the roots are growing out of the bottom of the pot, just nip them off.

Bonsai should be on a schedule of regular fertilization from the beginning of April until the end of June, when the strength should be reduced to fifty percent until the end of September. If a plant goes dormant during this period of intense heat, immediately discontinue fertilizing; for other plants, discontinue regular fertilizing around the first of October, after which a low-nitrogen fertilizer may be given up to November first. All fertilization should be stopped before December.

In the Southwest, junipers can be collected during the hot summer months, since some varieties go dormant then; but this requires utmost care with the root ball, so the root system is not disturbed. Other trees might be collected during January and February, if they are dormant; but if in doubt, wait until early spring.

Depending on the elevation and how far inland the location is, winter activities for the bonsai grower in this region can include repotting. In Texas, repotting can begin at the end of December and continue into January. During this period, maintaining sufficient moisture is the biggest problem for the bonsai grower.

Most of the Southwest can experience hot desert winds with low humidity; therefore, watering is extremely important. At higher elevations there can be an occasional freeze, so growers must be prepared. The beginner in this region should check with local growers to find out what types of plant material will survive within these microenvironments.

Some good bonsai materials native to the Southwest are:

sweet gum, *Liquidambar styraciflua*
chinaberry, *Melia azedarach*
tamarisk, *Tamarix parviflora*
Atlas cedar, *Cedrus atlantica*
deodar cedar, *Cedrus deodara*
cedar of Lebanon, *Cedrus libani*
oleander, *Nerium oleander*
privet, *Ligustrum* spp.
azalea, *Rhododendron* spp.
olive, *Olea europaea*
Rosemary, *Rosmarinus officinalis*
California juniper, *Juniperus californica*
pomegranate, *Punica granatum*
Hollywood juniper, *Juniperus chinensis* var. *torulosa*

THE ROCKY MOUNTAIN AND GREAT PLAINS REGION

The Rocky Mountains extend from northern Alaska to central New Mexico and also cover sections of the Yukon Territory, the Northwest Territories, British Columbia, Alberta, Montana, Idaho, Wyoming, Nevada, Utah, Colorado, and Arizona. There are four climatic zones within this region, with altitudes ranging from 2,000 to 14,000 feet. The midpoint of this region is Denver, Colorado: the growing seasons shorten as one moves north or to higher elevations, and lengthen as one moves south or to lower elevations.

The most northern area of this region covers British Columbia, Alberta, Montana, Idaho, and Wyoming. Altitudes range from 3,000 to 9,000 feet, and growing seasons are relatively short, except in low valleys. The central area of this region covers Nevada, Utah, and the western two-thirds of Colorado, with altitudes ranging from 4,000 to 14,000 feet. The growing season in this area varies considerably in number of days, and temperatures generally range from 90°F (about 32°C) in summer to -20°F (roughly -29°C) in winter.

The Great Plains extend from Alberta and Saskatchewan through the Dakotas to central Texas, with weather generally characterized by low humidity and high winds. The temperatures usually range from 100°F (almost 38°C) in summer to -40°F (-40°C) in the northern section during winter. The growing season in this area can often be long.

The high mountain areas, from the Selkirk and Monashee mountain ranges in Canada southward to the Sangre de Christo Mountains in New Mexico, have altitudes that range from 6,000 to 11,000 feet. In these areas, temperatures can easily dip to -30°F (roughly -34.5°C) or -40°F (-40°C); and in winter plants suffer not only from the cold but also from dryness and the hot sun.

If plants need it, repotting can be started when spring arrives: around mid-March in the Denver area, about a week later at higher elevations, and some two or three weeks later well to the north. Also, fertilizing of those plants that are not repotted is begun at this time, and some pruning of flowering bonsai can be done after they have finished blooming.

In general, summers in this region are characterized by bright sun, dry air, and temperatures up to 90°F (about 32°C) or 100°F (almost 38°C). Night temperatures can dip to 50°F (10°C) or 60°F (about 15.5°C). In late spring and early summer, some protection may be necessary for newly repotted bonsai. Bonsai must be checked daily for dryness.

In this region, fall may come as early as September and may be accompanied by great fluctuations between daytime and nighttime temperatures. There are days where the sunny daytime temperature reaches 60°F (about 15.5°C); however, after sunset, it sometimes drops to 0°F (almost -18°C) and to -20°F (roughly -29°C) by midnight. Under such conditions, bonsai roots may be damaged, so growers should be prepared to cover the bonsai or to move them indoors.

During winter, bonsai in this region need protection from the middle of September to the middle of March. One system that seems to work well is to bury the trees in gravel beds to protect the root systems from the great extremes in temperature. Cold frames or greenhouses can also be used.

Many different plants in this region can be used for bonsai, since there is a cold period that allows the temperate plants to go dormant. Indeed, this region abounds in natural material that can be collected for bonsai, including:

juniper, *Juniperus* spp.
spruce, *Picea* spp.
pine, *Pinus* spp.
yew, *Taxus* spp.
larch, *Larix* spp.
hackberry, *Celtis reticulata*
eastern redbud, *Cercis canadensis*
hawthorn, *Crataegus* spp.
apple, *Malus* spp.
flowering quince, *Chaenomeles* spp.
maple, *Acer* spp.

Two trees native to this region—the Rocky Mountain juniper, *Juniperus scopulorum,* and the ponderosa pine, *Pinus ponderosa*—are often collected and used as bonsai by noted bonsai collectors in the United States.

THE PACIFIC NORTHWEST AND BRITISH COLUMBIA

This region borders the Pacific and has many inlets and valleys that have temperatures much like those of Japan. Extending from northern California to Alaska and from the far western slopes of the Rocky Mountains to the Pacific Ocean, the region is warmed by the North Pacific, Japan, and Alaska currents, which produce a moderate climate and long growing seasons. Broadly speaking, there are four major areas in this region: the exposed coastal strip, ranging from 300 growing days in the south to 225 in the north; the Seattle-Vancouver area, where the growing season is from 150 to 250 days, with moderate summer temperatures; the area from Portland to northern California, which has a growing season of 200 to 300 days, with heat and dryness in the summers but with winters free from extreme cold; and the interior area, a great fruit-producing section of America, where winters are relatively mild, with some snow and late spring frosts.

Bonsai care for this part of North America must be divided into two sections because areas in British Columbia, Washington, and Oregon that are west of the Cascade Range have a climate that is very different from that found in areas east of the Cascade Range. Winters east of these mountains are severe and growers there should refer to the section on the Rocky Mountain region for their information. West of the Cascade Range the winters are mild, often without any snow, and the temperature rarely goes below 28°F (about -2°C) in winter.

Spring in the Pacific northwest follows the coastline northward from the south so that weather along the coast may be springlike in January, although inland areas may wait until April for spring, depending upon fluctuations of weather. Hardy bonsai in areas west of the mountains are left on the display benches during the winter; but one must be alert to sudden changes in the weather during this time, since arctic air may pour in, accompanied by dry north and northeast winds that can desiccate plants.

Dormant pruning of deciduous trees can be done in January and February, since many species of plants will bloom from late January to March and April. Fertilizing should begin in April for plants that are not to be repotted, and of course, repotting can start as soon as plants show signs of bud formation.

Summers in the area west of the Cascade Range do not have prolonged periods of hot weather, so summer care can be more relaxed than elsewhere in the country. However, watering is necessary at all times during the summer. One species of tree that needs fogging with a mist nozzle during the summer months is the alpine fir (*Abies lasiocarpa*), because it apparently draws moisture in through its needles and responds well to fogging. With maples and elms, constant nipping and pruning of new growth is necessary all summer in order to maintain shape.

Fall brings about a reduction in activities, beginning with the stopping of fertilizing in September and ending with the protection of less hardy trees by mulching them into the ground (just above the pot line or beneath low shrubs), where they are protected from the north wind. During fall and winter, that is, November through late January, the bonsai grower must be attentive to the weather reports; and if the prediction is for unusually cold weather, then tender bonsai need some additional protection.

Native plants used as bonsai in this region include:

maple, *Acer* spp.
European hornbeam, *Carpinus betulus*
European beech, *Fagus sylvatica*
ginkgo, *Ginkgo biloba*
sweet gum, *Liquidambar styraciflua*
flowering crab apple, *Malus* spp.
flowering cherry, plum, and apricot, *Prunus* spp.
various cedars, *Cedrus* spp.
false cypress, *Chamaecyparis* spp.
cryptomeria, *Cryptomeria japonica*

spruce, *Picea* spp.
various pines, *Pinus* spp.
hemlock, *Tsuga* spp.
quince, *Chaenomeles* spp.
enkianthus, *Enkianthus campanalatus*
azalea, *Rhododendron* spp.
Japanese stewartia, *Stewartia pseudocamellia maxim*

8. DISPLAYING BONSAI

BUILT into the formal living room of the traditional Japanese home is a *tokonoma,* or alcove, where art objects, to be viewed almost at eye level from low cushions on the floor, are displayed against a plain background of soft, subtle color. Items frequently placed in the tokonoma include a flower arrangement, a small planting of grasses or herbs, lacquer or bronze boxes, a curious stone, a particularly handsome piece of pottery, or a prized bonsai. Like the other objects, the bonsai is not on permanent display but is brought out on special occasions. Usually the tokonoma holds two or three objects. The display effect can be either formal or informal. A scroll may be hung in the center of the back wall of the tokonoma, with a bonsai positioned before it to the right or the left; the accent pieces are chosen for suitability—for a mood cool and delicate or bold and rugged.

The bonsai and any accessory pieces are often placed on separate wooden bases or stands, which are frequently crosscut slabs stained to emphasize the pattern of the grain. Or perhaps a small, lacquered table with gracefully curved legs or a polished base fashioned from tree roots will be used as a stand.

There are degrees of ornateness. Bases are always selected to match the mood of the bonsai. The base for a formal upright tree is also formal and extends a little beyond the feet of the container to give a solid, settled air. A dark-finished base increases the feeling of stability. Informal trees are displayed on simple bases of lighter appearance. If the bonsai is semicascading or cascading, it is placed on a tall stand to suggest a tree growing on a steep hill, with branches hanging down the side. There are no rules; each display reflects your own decorative taste. But emphasis is always on the bonsai; other objects must not detract from its importance.

American homes, so different from traditional Japanese homes, seem to present problems in displaying bonsai. In our living rooms it is difficult to find an eye-level space with a clear background. I use room dividers and sectional bookshelves, where the distance between shelves can be varied, to accommodate bonsai of small to medium size. A gray, off-white, gray-green, or even beige background will complement most bonsai. Coffee tables permit trees to be displayed in the round; but since they then offer no particular background, a bonsai is too often lost to view among household objects. Although the Japanese would probably frown on such a place of display, our American sense of decoration is not violated, so long as the character of a tree remains intact.

ACCENT PLANTS

Other plants—minute shrubs, herbs, grasses, or wildflowers—may accompany the bonsai. Miniature bonsai can be accents for larger trees, or for paintings, decorative boxes, or stones. But, as in the Japanese home, companion pieces to the bonsai must always complement the tree and not dominate it. It is the bonsai that is important. It should project a mood or feeling, or suggest a scene of nature reproduced in miniature. If the display communicates this, then you have accomplished your purpose.

In summer, trees are selected for their cool, serene appearance. Willows are appropriate for the main display, with a small stone or rock-planting in a separate container of sand and water as a companion piece. If a scroll is hung, it might be a scene of birds in flight against the sky. Keep the composition simple; create an illusion by understatement.

Accent plants are usually grown in small, shallow containers so they can be displayed clearly subordinate to the larger bonsai. Over the years I have experimented with various native American materials grown in small containers; and my plants have either been collected, with due regard for conservation practices, or purchased from nurseries specializing in wild and alpine plants.

Materials native to North America that make decorative accent plants include:
alpine azalea, *Rhododendron lapponicum*
alpine buttercup, *Ranunculus eschscholtzii*

American columbine, *Aquilegia canadensis*
bird's-foot violet, *Viola pedata*
blue-eyed grass, *Sisyrinchium* spp.
bluet, *Houstonia caerulea*
blue violet, *Viola sororio*
bunchberry, *Cornus canadensis*
downy rattlesnake plantain, *Goodyera pubescens*
gold-star grass, *Hypoxis hirsuta*
horsetail, *Equisetum* spp.
mountain cranberry, *Vaccinium vitis-idaea* var. *minus*
pasture rose, *Rosa carolina*
partridgeberry, *Mitchella repens*
pincushion plant, *Diapensia lapponica*
shrubby cinquefoil, *Potentilla fruticosa*
small ferns, such as the Christmas fern, *Polypodium vulgare*
spleenworts, *Asplenium* spp.
trailing arbutus, *Epigaea repens*
Virginia saxifrage, *Saxifraga virginiensis*
woodland (white) aster, *Aster divaricatus*
wintergreen, *Gaultheria procumbens*
yellow violet, *Viola rotundifolia*

These small plantings need to be watered carefully in hot weather, when they dry out quickly. In summer, I keep them on trays of moist sand in places that are partially shaded in the afternoon. Because of the small amount of soil in each container, the plants that grow rapidly, such as bluet, horsetail, and aster, must be repotted every year if they are to remain in peak condition. The best time to repot is just after the plants have bloomed or early in the spring.

DISPLAYING BONSAI OUTDOORS

In summer, bonsai can be displayed in various ways in the garden or on the patio. Since bonsai are living forms of sculpture, they can be used in the same way as other pieces of garden sculpture. Bonsai are most decorative when they are placed attractively in a definite setting and not simply clustered on tables to facilitate their care.

I think of one display in particular, in a home with a living-room picture

126. Bonsai displayed at a private home. The benches are made from ceramic drain tiles and rough planks.

window that looks out on a white stone-and-gravel garden. Silhouetted against the whiteness is a collection of fifteen or so small to medium-sized bonsai pleasantly grouped on a table at window height.

In another setting, individual bonsai are placed on stones and tree stumps in the garden, like pieces of sculpture. The beauty of each bonsai is clearly seen, yet all blend into the harmonious garden composition. Such an arrangement, however, depends on both site and suitable stands to support and display the plants.

EXHIBITING AND JUDGING

Public exhibits of bonsai are always well attended. In the past in America, these exhibits have been held mainly in botanical gardens; but with the rapid formation of societies devoted to bonsai, there has been a considerable increase in the number of public shows. Local garden clubs have become interested in bonsai, and their smaller shows frequently include one or more classes for bonsai, even though there have been problems in exhibiting such unusual material. Plants in competition require judging, and it has been difficult to set standards for bonsai. Furthermore, the usual means of display hardly suffice for bonsai.

Vinciguerra

127. Staging at the Philadelphia Flower and Garden Show. Courtesy of the Pennsylvania Horticultural Society.

In Japan, public exhibitions are held in all seasons and each show has a different set of fixtures. In general, bonsai are exhibited on long tables and are separated from each other by dividers. Sometimes these dividers are fairly elaborate, so that each entry is seen in its own alcove; and sometimes the dividers are simply pieces of board a few inches high, colored to match the background. Each entry is usually given four to six feet of space on a table about four feet high.

Also on display are the accompaniments of bonsai: bases, stands, scrolls, stones, boxes, and accessory plantings—all the various objects found in the Japanese tokonoma. Tables, walls, and dividers are of a light, neutral color, to complement the various types of trees exhibited.

Japanese shows are frequently sponsored by commercial bonsai associations, and the display equipment is permanent. In America, we rarely have such desirable conditions. The space for bonsai in American flower shows is almost always limited and inadequate for proper display. However, it is usually possible to have a blank wall for background and to cover it with some light fabric, monk's cloth, burlap, or even seamless paper. On the standard, waist-high display tables, bonsai are placed on boxes to elevate them to a more appropriate viewing level. Small and miniature bonsai are best displayed on raised stands to bring them even higher.

128. The Rosade Bonsai Studio display at the Philadelphia Flower and Garden Show. Courtesy of the Rosade Bonsai Studio, New Hope, Pennsylvania.

PROBLEMS OF JUDGING

With regard to judging, there are no traditional Japanese sources to consult: the Japanese do not ordinarily judge their shows (with the exception of azaleas). In Japan bonsai are exhibited and appreciated for their beauty: they are not in competition. Each owner displays his tree as if it were a work of art in a gallery.

In America, most bonsai societies follow this practice in their own shows, concentrating only on the display. Lack of competition seems to stimulate interest; at least it does not reduce it, perhaps because a bonsai partakes of art as well as of horticulture. Standards for horticulture can be completely objective, but this is not so with art.

Exhibitions avoid the ever-increasing difficulty of competitions, in which we must answer the question of whether it is fair to allow a purchased tree, designed and created by a professional artist, to compete against a tree developed by an amateur. If such competition is not fair how can we include the professional examples of bonsai in amateur exhibits? Certainly the beauty and teaching value of bonsai created by a master are important. In Japan, more often than not, a famous tree has one creator and a different owner; but since the shows there are art exhibits and not horticultural contests, there is no problem. Perhaps the difficulty can be overcome by requiring professional bonsai to be only *exhibited* and not entered in competition. We then need to establish definite criteria for what is professional and what is amateur. I suggest that if a bonsai is *not* trained by the exhibitor, it should be placed in a special noncompetitive class or exhibit.

Judging the Style

Plants in competition are first judged as to basic style:
Formal upright, with a straight trunk, top erect;
Informal upright, with the trunk slightly curved, top bent toward the front;
Slanting style, with the trunk slanted or curved to either the left or right, the lowest branch spreading in the direction opposite the bend in the main trunk, top bent slightly forward;
Semicascading, with the trunk growing straight up from the soil and then turning sharply downward, the tip of the main trunk reaching below the rim of the container;
Cascading, with the trunk growing as in the semicascading style, but the tip of the trunk reaching below the feet of the container.
In considering the style of bonsai, the judge must be aware of the many variations and substyles that are in some degree based on the five basic styles. In *The Japanese Art of Miniature Trees and Landscapes,* Yoshimura and Halford list four groups of styles. Group one contains sixteen styles of single-trunk trees, classified according to the shape of the trunk; group two, five styles featuring multiple trunks from a single root; group three, eight styles of group plantings, each with two or more separate trees; group four, three styles of group plantings that are not bonsai in the strict sense.

Judging the Front

The second consideration for the judge is whether the bonsai is displayed with its front turned toward the viewer. If so, in the case of upright and slanting trees, the lower branches will form a distinct triad pattern—two branches trained forward (one of them slightly higher, on the better side), with the third branch between or above the first two and extending toward the back of the tree to give depth to the overall composition. If a bonsai is displayed backwards, the branches seen are well developed and hide the line of the trunk, which should be the center of interest. The branch arrangement should be complimentary to the trunk.

ARTISTIC MERIT

Next, the judge considers the general artistic effect, specifically:
  Suitability of the style to the natural form of the species;
  Design of the lower trunk and surface roots;
  Relative proportions of branches, twigs, flowers, fruits, and leaves or needles
    to the trunk and to each other;
  Harmony of surface underplanting with the style and composition;
  Relation of container to the shape and color of the tree;
  Display effect of the base on the composition;
  Technique of pruning and wiring, noting especially any wire marks on trunk
    and branches.
  If a point system is used in judging, then style, front, and general artistic effect count for at least fifty percent. Finally, quality of horticulture is examined, and this counts for the other fifty points. To be considered here are:
  General health;
  Condition and color of leaves or needles, branches, flowers, and fruit;
  Health of the underplanting.
  These, then, are the main elements in judging bonsai. Techniques for developing bonsai are more complicated than those in the culture of other plants, and so judging bonsai is more difficult. Culture itself is also more difficult. Study, especially under an accomplished master, and reading help; but these alone will not lead to competence. This comes with constant practice and, more important, with close observation of bonsai acknowledged to be masterpieces of their models—the *natural* forms of trees.
  For anyone who wishes to learn more about judging bonsai, the American Bonsai Society has published a *Bonsai Manual* for appreciating, judging, and buying bonsai. This manual can be purchased from the Society for $3.50 per copy by writing to the address given below.

Some bonsai clubs in the United States to which a beginner might write for information and to find out about local clubs are:

American Bonsai Society
228 Rosemont Avenue
Erie, Pennsylvania 16505

Bonsai Clubs International
P.O. Box 2098
Sunnyvale, California 94087

The California Bonsai Society, Inc.
P.O. Box 78211
Los Angeles, California 90016

The Bonsai Society of Greater New York
Box 343
New Hyde Park, New York 11040

Public gardens or arboretums where bonsai are on public display include:

Arnold Arboretum
The Arborway
Jamaica Plains, Massachusetts 02130

Brooklyn Botanic Garden
1000 Washington Avenue
Brooklyn, New York 11225

Duke Gardens Foundations, Inc.
Route 206 South
Somerville, New Jersey 08876

Longwood Gardens
Kennett Square, Pennsylvania 19348

U.S. National Arboretum
R Street at 24th St., N.E. (off Bladensburg Rd.)
Washington, D.C. 20002

George Landis Arboretum
Esperance, New York 12066

BONSAI RECORD

Date Acquired _____

BOTANICAL NAME _____

COMMON NAME _____

NAME AND ADDRESS OF SOURCE _____

ACQUIRED AS BONSAI _____ PARTIALLY TRAINED _____ UNTRAINED _____ COLLECTED TREE _____ COST _____

AGE WHEN ACQUIRED: Actual _____ Estimated _____ SEEDLING _____ CUTTING _____ GRAFT _____ OTHER _____

SIZE: Height _____ Spread _____ NO. TRUNKS _____ TRUNK DIAMETER _____ STYLE _____

CONDITION AT TIME ACQUIRED _____

DATE _____ TREATMENT* _____

*Fertilizing, Wiring, Removing Wire, Repotting, Leaf Trimming, Pruning, Spraying, Restyling, Photographing

DATE _____ TREATMENT* _____

DATE _____ SHOW OR EXHIBIT _____ COMMENT _____

©The American Bonsai Society 1967

BONSAI RECORDS

ROSADE BONSAI STUDIO
BOX 303, ELY RD. RD 1, NEW HOPE, PA. 18938
(215) 862 9925

Date acquired _____

BOTANICAL NAME _____

JAPANESE NAME _____

COMMON NAME _____

NAME & ADDRESS of SOURCE _____

ACQUIRED AS: BONSAI ____ trained ____ partially trained ____ untrained ____
COLLECTED TREE ____ NURSERY STOCK ____ COST ____

AGE WHEN ACQUIRED ____ yrs. ____ Estimated ____ Actual ____

CREATED FROM: Seed ____ Cutting ____ Graft ____ Airlayer ____ Seedling ____ Other ____

SIZE: Height ____ Spread ____ No. trunks ____ Trunk dia. ____ Style ____

CONDITION AT TIME ACQUIRED: Potted ____ Canned ____ Bare root ____ B & B ____

Excellent ____ Good ____ Fair ____ Poor ____

Remarks: _____

Date of Repot	TREATMENT	Potting mix/additives

Date of Repot	TREATMENT	Potting mix/additives

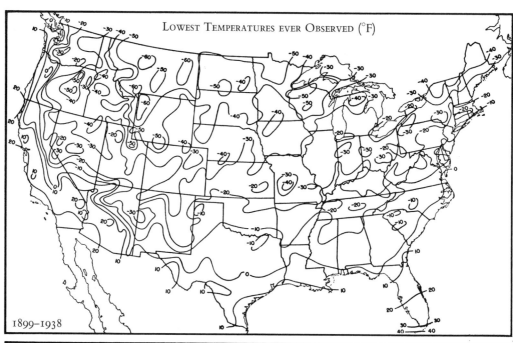

LOWEST TEMPERATURES EVER OBSERVED (°F)

1899–1938

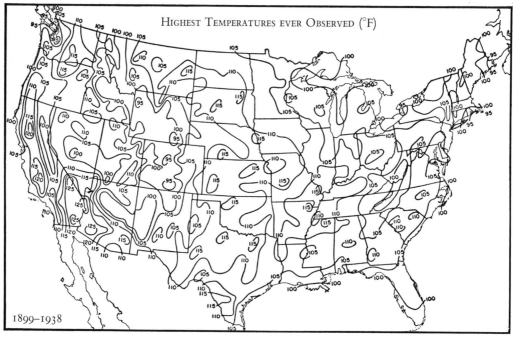

HIGHEST TEMPERATURES EVER OBSERVED (°F)

1899–1938

TEMPERATURE EXTREMES IN THE UNITED STATES

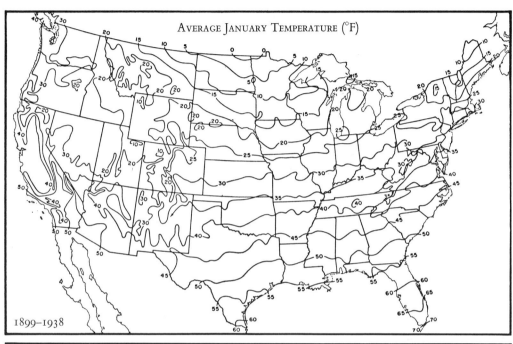

Average January Temperature (°F)

1899–1938

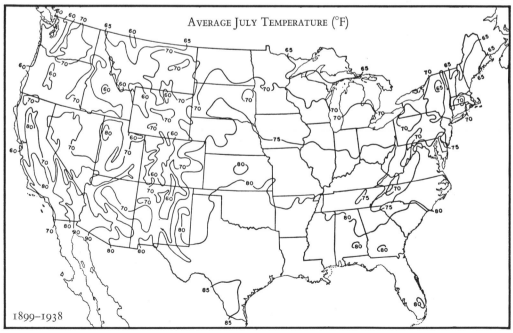

Average July Temperature (°F)

1899–1938

POTTING SCHEDULE

	Northeast North-Central Region & Adjacent Canada	The Southeast & the Gulf Region	The Southwest & Most of California	Rocky Mountain & Great Plains Region	Pacific Northwest & British Columbia
JAN					
FEB					
MAR					
APR					
MAY					
JUN					
JUL					
AUG					
SEP					
OCT					
NOV					
DEC					

give bonsai winter protection   give bonsai shade in summer

acclimate trees for spring or winter conditions   best time to transplant bonsai

1. Plants that should be repotted just before new buds appear in the spring:

gardenia	beech	hawthorn
Ilex spp.	crab apple	crape myrtle
hornbeam	cherry	serviceberry
ivy	cotoneaster	larch
	zelkova and elm species	Chinese quince

2. Plants that should be repotted after new buds appear in spring:

black pine	maple	yew
white pine	red pine	ginko
spruce	pomegranate	hemlock
cryptomeria	needle juniper	barberry
	Chinese juniper	

3. Plants that should be transplanted after flowering:

magnolia	*Prunus* spp.	camellia
	azalea	wisteria

4. Plants that should be transplanted before flowering:
winter jasmine, either spring or fall

5. Plant species that should be transplanted in fall:
Japanese quince

SHAPING SCHEDULES FOR NORTH AMERICA

WIRING AND SHAPING SCHEDULE

	Northeast North-Central Region & Adjacent Canada	The Southeast & the Gulf Region	The Southwest & Most of California	Rocky Mountain & Great Plains Region	Pacific Northwest & British Columbia
Jan					
Feb					
Mar					
Apr					
May					
Jun					
Jul					
Aug					
Sep					
Oct					
Nov					
Dec					

wire and shape deciduous plants

wire and shape evergreen plants

allow bonsai to make growth (in spring) or to become dormant (as fall and winter approach)

1. Plants that should be wired and shaped before new buds appear in spring:

black pine	red pine	gardenia (spring or summer)
cotoneaster	hemlock	Chinese quince

2. Plants that should be wired and shaped just as new buds appear:

Wisteria

3. Plants that should be wired and shaped in late fall or winter:

White pine   spruce

4. Plants that should be wired and shaped after spring bud-pinching:

cherry	elm	crab apple
Ilex spp.	hornbeam	crape myrtle
magnolia	beech	apricot
	needle juniper hawthorn	

5. Plants that should be wired and shaped during the growing season (never remove wires in winter, since cracking the cambium layer will kill the branch):

all azaleas

APPENDIX D

NORTH AMERICAN HARDINESS ZONES AND GROWING REGIONS

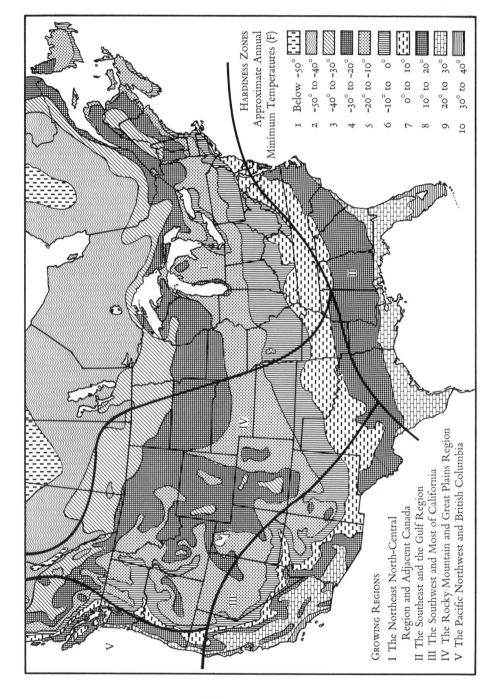

HARDINESS ZONES
Approximate Annual
Minimum Temperatures (F)

1	Below −50°
2	−50° to −40°
3	−40° to −30°
4	−30° to −20°
5	−20° to −10°
6	−10° to 0°
7	0° to 10°
8	10° to 20°
9	20° to 30°
10	30° to 40°

GROWING REGIONS
I The Northeast North-Central
  Region and Adjacent Canada
II The Southeast and the Gulf Region
III The Southwest and Most of California
IV The Rocky Mountain and Great Plains Region
V The Pacific Northwest and British Columbia

APPENDIX E

NORTH AMERICAN BONSAI MATERIALS
GROUPED BY SIMILARITIES IN GROWTH HABITS

I. Evergreens suitable for bonsai from the genera *Abies, Cedrus, Chamaecyparis, Juniperus, Larix, Picea, Pinus, Pseudotsuga, Tsuga,* and *Taxus.*

Abies lasiocarpa, alpine fir

TRANSPLANT: In spring.
PRUNE: In spring, pinching out any unnecessary new shoots before they harden and leaving only a few needles at the base of each shoot retained.
WIRE: Any time except while buds are soft.

Abies firma, Japanese fir

TRANSPLANT: In spring.
PRUNE: Trim several times in spring, breaking off or pinching out new shoots before they harden and leaving only a few needles at the base of each shoot.
WIRE: Any time except when buds are soft.

Abies sachalinensis, Sakhalin fir

TRANSPLANT: In spring.
PRUNE: Pinch out new buds at any time during the growing season; wait until side buds appear next to the new twigs, then pinch out the buds when these new twigs have grown too long, leaving one or two side buds.
WIRE: Any time except when buds are soft.

Cedrus deodara, deodar cedar
TRANSPLANT: In spring.

Cedrus libani, cedar of Lebanon

PRUNE: Pinch out or pull the tops off the new buds at any time during the growing season.

WIRE: Any time.

Chamaecyparis spp., white cedar   *Chamaecyparis thyoides,* Atlantic white cedar
Chamaecyparis obtusa, hinoki   *Chamaecyparis obtusa nana,* dwarf *hinoki*
                Chamaecyparis pisifera, sawara cypress

TRANSPLANT: In early spring.

PRUNE: Spring to autumn, when new buds appear; vigorously prune twice in spring and once in fall.

WIRE: In early spring.

Juniperus californica, California juniper   *Juniperus monosperma,* one-seed juniper
Juniperus communis, common juniper   *Juniperus rigida,* needle juniper
Juniperus scopulorum, Rocky Mountain juniper   *Juniperus virginiana,* eastern red cedar
Juniperus conferta, shore juniper   *Juniperus chinensis,* Chinese juniper
                Juniperus squamata wilsonii, prostrate juniper

TRANSPLANT: In spring, when new buds begin to appear.

PRUNE: As new buds appear. Repeat during the growing season.

WIRE: Old branches in spring, before new buds appear; new shoots, after they have hardened.

Larix leptolepsis, Japanese larch

TRANSPLANT: In early spring, before buds sprout.

PRUNE: Pinch out new buds at any time during the growing season; wait until side buds appear next to the new twigs, then pinch out the buds when these new twigs have grown too long, leaving one or two side buds.

WIRE: Any time except while new buds are soft. Use wire wrapped in paper.

Larix decidua, European larch   *Larix laricina,* American larch
Taxodium distichum, bald cypress   *Sequoia sempervirens,* redwood

TRANSPLANT: In spring, before buds sprout.

PRUNE: Wait until side buds appear; pinch out, leaving one or two side buds.

WIRE: In spring or summer, except when new buds are soft.

Picea jezoensis, Ezo spruce   *Picea abies nidiformis,* pond's nest spruce
Picea glauca conica, Alberta spruce   *Picea omorika,* Serbian spruce

TRANSPLANT: In spring, when the buds begin to come out.

PRUNE: Pinch out as shoots grow long: every two or three days over a two-week period.

WIRE: Major branches and trunk during winter; new twigs, after they have hardened in late spring.

Pinus mugo, mugho pine   *Pinus nigra,* Austrian pine
Pinus densiflora, red pine   *Pinus rigida,* pitch pine
Pinus thunbergii, Japanese black pine   *Pinus thunbergii corticosa,* cork bark pine
Pinus echinata, shortleaf pine   *Pinus ponderosa,* ponderosa pine
Pinus sylvestris, Scotch pine   *Pinus virginiana,* Virginia pine

TRANSPLANT: In spring, after buds appear.

PRUNE: In spring. On pines, buds should be pinched out rather closely, leaving only three or four bundles of needles at the base of each shoot. After about a month or so, two or three secondary shoots will begin to appear from the bases of old buds. Because secondary buds appear, these shoots will not grow too long and both branches and needles will become smaller. In fall, around September, shorten branches and remove old needles.

WIRE: In spring, before buds come out.

Pinus parviflora, Japanese white pine   *Pinus strobus nana,* dwarf white pine

TRANSPLANT: In late spring.

PRUNE: Pinch only the tips of the buds. In September remove old needles.

WIRE: In winter.

Pseudotsuga taxifolia, Douglas fir   *Tsuga sieboldii,* Japanese hemlock
Tsuga canadensis, eastern hemlock   *Tsuga diversifolia,* northern hemlock
Thuja occidentalis, northern white cedar

TRANSPLANT: In spring, as buds appear.

PRUNE: After needles have hardened somewhat.

WIRE: Any time in spring except as new shoots emerge.

Taxus cuspidata, Japanese yew   *Taxus baccata,* English yew

TRANSPLANT: In spring.

PRUNE: Pinch out new growth any time during the growing season.

WIRE: Any time except while new buds emerge.

Cryptomeria japonica, cryptomeria

TRANSPLANT: In early spring.

PRUNE: During the growing season; repeat several times. Use fingertips, not shears.

WIRE: In early spring, just before budding.

II. Deciduous plants suitable for bonsai from among maples, elms, and genera with similar habits.

Acer rubrum, red maple   *Acer buergerianum,* trident maple

Acer palmatum, Japanese maple   *Acer palmatum dissectum,* cut-leaf maple
Rhus succedanea, wax tree

TRANSPLANT: In spring, as buds appear.
PRUNE: Pinch out terminal buds after shoots have three or four nodes, leaving only two nodes. Pinch out lateral buds and secondary buds, leaving only one node.
WIRE: After leaves and shoots have hardened. Use wire wrapped in paper.

Lagerstroemia indica, crape myrtle

TRANSPLANT: In spring, as buds begin to show.
PRUNE: Pinch off new buds after flower buds appear or after flowering. Trim branches in the fall.
WIRE: In midsummer, after shoots have hardened. Use wire wrapped in paper.

Elaeagnus multiflora, cherry elaeagnus

TRANSPLANT: In spring, as buds come out.
PRUNE: After blossoms appear and before new buds harden, in the later part of summer.
WIRE: From spring into summer.

Ulmus alata, winged elm   *Ulmus americana,* American elm
Ulmus crassifolia, cedar elm   *Ulmus pumila,* Siberian elm
Zelkova serrata, Japanese gray-bark elm

TRANSPLANT: In spring, before buds come out.
PRUNE: After leaves have come out. Main buds: leave four or five nodes out of six or seven. Secondary buds: leave two or three nodes out of four or five. Pinch two or three times in early spring.
WIRE: Shoots in spring, as they harden. Turn shoots upward.

Celtis occidentalis, hackberry

TRANSPLANT: In spring, as buds appear.
PRUNE: Trim after the new shoots lengthen to three to five nodes during the growing season; leave one or two nodes.
WIRE: Spring to summer, after shoots harden. Use wire wrapped in paper.

Ginkgo biloba, ginkgo

TRANSPLANT: In spring, when the new buds appear as dots of green.
PRUNE: Terminal buds should be shortened to two or three nodes when leaves have hardened. Secondary buds should be pinched, leaving two or three nodes out of four or five. Pinch off unnecessary buds.
WIRE: Do not wire.

Salix babylonica, weeping willow

TRANSPLANT: In spring or midsummer.

PRUNE: Trim to three or four nodes at time of transplanting. Allow all new shoots to grow without pinching and remove buds not necessary for design.
WIRE: Only thick branches, in early spring before buds come out. Watch wires closely because this species grows rapidly.

III. Deciduous plants suitable for bonsai from the Rosaceae family.

Hamamelis virginiana, southern witch hazel   *Hamamelis vernalis,* common witch hazel
Hamamelis japonica, Japanese witch hazel
TRANSPLANT: In early spring, before leaf buds open.
PRUNE: Trim in midsummer, after the leaves harden.
WIRE: In spring, before buds open.

Liquidambar styraciflua, sweet gum   *Styrax japonica,* Japanese snowbell
TRANSPLANT: In early spring, as new buds appear.
PRUNE: Trim after the leaves harden.
WIRE: In midsummer, after new growth has become woody.

Amelanchier spp, serviceberry   *Amelanchier asiatica,* Japanese serviceberry
TRANSPLANT: In spring, before buds appear.
PRUNE: Trim after flowering. Let leaves harden and pinch off tips of shoots.
WIRE: In midsummer, after new growth has become woody.

Crataegus oxyacantha, English hawthorn   *Crataegus cuneata,* Japanese hawthorn
TRANSPLANT: In early spring, as buds appear.
PRUNE: Trim in midsummer, after the blossoms wither and before new buds harden.
WIRE: Spring to summer, as new wood hardens.

Chaenomeles sinensis, Chinese quince
TRANSPLANT: In spring, before buds come out.
PRUNE: Shorten all shoots as leaves harden, leaving only one or two nodes. Secondary buds are pinched in the same way. Remove unnecessary buds before they develop.
WIRE: Older branches can be shaped in early spring before buds come out. Use wire wrapped in paper.

Cydonia oblonga, common quince
TRANSPLANT: In spring, as flower buds begin to swell.
PRUNE: After flowers have withered and as new shoots harden.
WIRE: In spring or after shoots have become woody.

Chaenomeles spp., Japanese flowering quince
TRANSPLANT: In late summer or early fall.
PRUNE: During the growing season. Trim long shoots back to two or three nodes.
WIRE: Any time except winter.

Malus angustifolia, southern crab apple   *Malus coronaria,* sweet crab apple
Malus fusca, Oregon crab apple   *Malus ioensis,* prairie crab apple
Malus pumila, common apple   *Malus halliana,* Hall's crab apple
Malus parkmanii, Parkman crab apple   *Malus micromalus,* midget crab apple
TRANSPLANT: In early spring, as buds begin to appear.
PRUNE: After shoots have lengthened. Trim back to two or three nodes.
WIRE: At the time of transplanting or in midsummer, after new shoots have become woody.

Prunus japonica, flowering almond   *Prunus maritima,* beach plum
Prunus mume, Japanese flowering apricot
The *Prunus* genus includes both ornamentals and fruiting species (e.g., plums, apricots, almonds, peaches, and cherries). Cultivation is the same for most species.
TRANSPLANT: In spring, after flowering.
PRUNE: After the new buds have appeared and shoots have lengthened. Leave the new shoots until late summer, then trim, leaving one or two nodes.
WIRE: At the time of trimming. Use wire wrapped in paper.

Pyrus communis, pear   *Sorbus* spp., mountain ash
Cercis canadensis, eastern redbud   *Cercis chinensis,* Chinese redbud
TRANSPLANT: In early spring, as flower buds appear.
PRUNE: Trim after shoots have lengthened, leaving two or three nodes. Trim tips after the leaves have hardened.
WIRE: After shoots have begun to harden. Use wire wrapped in paper.

Gleditsia triacanthos, honey locust
TRANSPLANT: In spring, as shoots appear.
PRUNE: After blossoms appear. Trim shoots that have lengthened, leaving one or two nodes.
WIRE: Midsummer to fall, as shoots harden.

IV. Deciduous plants suitable for bonsai from the Betulaceae and Fagaceae families.

Betula nigra, river birch   *Betula papyrifera,* paper birch
Betula populifolia, gray birch   *Betula platyphylla* var. *japonica,* Japanese white birch

TRANSPLANT: In early spring, as new leaves begin to appear.
PRUNE: After new shoots have lengthened to five to seven nodes, during the growing season; leave one or two nodes.
WIRE: After shoots have hardened. Use wire wrapped in paper.

Carpinus caroliniana, American hornbeam   *Carpinus japonica,* Japanese hornbeam
Carpinus betulus, European hornbeam   *Carpinus laxiflora,* loose-flowering hornbeam
Corylopsis spicata, winter hazel   *Ostrya virginiana,* hop hornbeam
TRANSPLANT: In spring, before buds come out.
PRUNE: In early spring prune to shape, after shoots have lengthened. Repeat if necessary until summer.
WIRE: Shape as shoots harden, in midsummer.

Fagus grandifolia, American beech   *Fagus crenata,* Japanese beech
Fagus sylvatica, European beech
TRANSPLANT: In spring, before buds come out.
PRUNE: Pinch new shoots while still soft, leaving only one or two nodes.
WIRE: In spring, as twigs harden. Use wire wrapped in paper. Remove wire within three months.

Quercus agrifolia, California live oak   *Quercus chrysolepis,* canyon live oak
Quercus dumosa, California scrub oak   *Quercus virginiana,* live oak
TRANSPLANT: In spring, just as buds break.
PRUNE: Trim the shoots after they lengthen, removing all but two or three nodes.
WIRE: After new shoots become woody.

Quercus macrocarpa, mossycup oak   *Quercus palustris,* pin oak
Quercus phellos, willow oak   *Quercus dentata,* daimyo oak
TRANSPLANT: In early spring, before the new buds break their casings.
PRUNE: Trim the shoots after they lengthen, removing all but two or three nodes.
WIRE: For shaping, after the new shoots become woody, in midsummer.

V. Evergreens and deciduous plants suitable for bonsai from the Ericaceae, Theaceae, Araliceae, and Rubiaceae families.

Andromeda spp., bog rosemary   *Pieris japonica,* Lily-of-the-Valley bush
Andromeda polifolia cvs. "montana," "angustifolia," "compacta," "grandiflora compacta," "major," "minima," and "nana," bog rosemary
TRANSPLANT: In early spring, after flowers wither and as new buds appear.
PRUNE: After new buds harden. Leave only two or three leaves.

WIRE: Late spring to summer.

Calluna spp., heather (many cultivars)   *Erica* spp., heath (many cultivars)
TRANSPLANT: In early spring, as new growth appears.
PRUNE: As needed, pinch buds with thumbnail or use sharp scissors.
WIRE: Only woody branches.

Enkianthus perulatus and E. cernuus, enkianthus

TRANSPLANT: In early spring, as buds appear.
PRUNE: Trim with scissors after blossoms wither and before shoots harden.
WIRE: In midsummer, as shoots become woody.

Kalmia latifolia, mountain laurel   *Kalmia angustifolia,* sheep laurel
TRANSPLANT: In late spring, after flowers wither and as new leaf buds appear.
PRUNE: After new shoots harden. Leave only two or three leaves.
WIRE: Late spring to summer, after shoots harden.

Rhododendron spp.

This group of evergreen, semievergreen, and deciduous shrubs and small trees has many
cultivars and includes both azaleas and rhododendron.
TRANSPLANT: In late spring, after flowers begin to wither.
PRUNE: After shoots have hardened. Leave only two or three leaves.
WIRE: Older branches in spring, before buds come out; new growth in midsummer with
wire wrapped in paper. To make wood more flexible, dry out soil one day before wiring.

Camellia japonica, camellia   *Camellia sasanqua,* sasanqua camellia
Stewartia pseudocamellia maxim, Japanese stewartia

TRANSPLANT: In spring, after flowering, or in fall depending on the genus. Transplant
Stewartia before its leaves come out.
PRUNE: The tips, after leaves have hardened.
WIRE: As soon as shoots are woody. Use wire wrapped in paper.

Hedera helix, English ivy

TRANSPLANT: In spring, before buds appear.
PRUNE: As shoots harden, trim them back to two or three leaves.
WIRE: At time of transplanting or when shoots have become woody. Use wire wrapped
in paper.

Gardenia jasminoides, cape jasmine   *Gardenia jasminoides* var. *radicans,* gardenia
Serissa foetida, serissa

TRANSPLANT: In late spring, as new buds appear. Keep warm in winter.

PRUNE: After blossoms appear. After shoots have lengthened to three or five nodes, trim back to one or two.
WIRE: As shoots become woody, in midsummer, or in spring or summer before new buds appear. Use wire wrapped in paper.

VI. Additional flowering and fruiting deciduous plants suitable for bonsai.

Diospyros virginiana, American persimmon   *Diospyros kaki,* Japanese persimmon
Diospyros lotus, date plum
TRANSPLANT: In spring, before buds appear.
PRUNE: Pinch off all unnecessary shoots as soon as possible. Allow buds to lengthen. Trim as necessary to shape.
WIRE: When leaves have hardened. Use wire wrapped in paper. Remove wires in autumn.
MOISTURE REQUIREMENTS: *D. virginiana,* moist soil; *D. kaki,* intermediate soil; *D. lotus,* dry soil.

Punica granatum, pomegranate
TRANSPLANT: In spring, as new buds begin to open.
PRUNE: As new shoots lengthen, leaving one or two nodes. After secondary buds lengthen, pinch back to one node.
WIRE: At time of pinching. Use wire wrapped in paper.

Cotoneaster spp., cotoneaster
TRANSPLANT: In spring, before buds appear.
PRUNE: Trim long, overgrown shoots.
WIRE: In spring, before buds appear. Use wire wrapped in paper.

Magnolia soulangiana, saucer magnolia   *Magnolia stellata,* star magnolia
TRANSPLANT: After flowering, before leaves come out.
PRUNE: After shoots have lengthened and leaves have hardened. Allow time for brittle new green growth to turn brown.
WIRE: As shoots harden. Use wire wrapped in paper. Remove wires in autumn.

Jasminum nitidum, confederate jasmine   *Jasminum nudiflorum,* winter jasmine
Jasminum officinale, poet's jasmine
TRANSPLANT: In spring, before flowers come out, or in fall, after leaves drop.
PRUNE: All shoots before they become large.
WIRE: After shoots have hardened. Use wire wrapped in paper.

Wisteria floribunda, Japanese wisteria   *Wisteria sinensis,* Chinese wisteria

TRANSPLANT: In early spring, after flowering.

PRUNE: Trim with scissors after the blossoms wither but before the new buds harden, in the later part of summer.

WIRE: Wire and shape just as new buds appear.

NOTE: In summer keep these bonsai in a basin of water.

BIBLIOGRAPHY

American Bonsai Society. *Bonsai Journal* 10, no. 3 (fall, 1976).

Baker, George W. "Sifting Soils." *Bonsai Journal* 9, no. 3 (fall, 1975).

Behme, Robert Lee. *Bonsai, Saikei, and Bonkei.* New York: William Morrow and Company, Inc., 1969.

Brooklyn Botanic Garden. *Handbook on Bonsai: Special Techniques.* Brooklyn: Brooklyn Botanic Garden, 1966.

———. *Handbook on Dwarfed Potted Trees: The Bonsai of Japan.* Brooklyn: Brooklyn Botanic Garden, 1953.

Christopher, Everett P. *The Pruning Manual.* New York: The MacMillan Company, 1960.

Everett, T. H. *Living Trees of the World.* New York: Doubleday & Company, Inc., n.d.

Feininger, Andreas. *Trees.* New York: The Viking Press, 1968.

Kawamoto, Toshio. *Saikei: Living Landscapes in Miniature.* Tokyo, New York, and San Francisco: Kodansha International Ltd., 1967.

———, and Kurihara, Joseph Y. *Bonsai-Saikei: The Japanese Miniature Trees, Gardens, and Landscapes.* Tokyo: Nippon Saikei Co., 1963.

Kawasumi, Masakuni. *Bonsai with American Trees.* Tokyo, New York, and San Francisco: Kodansha International Ltd., 1975.

———. *Introductory Bonsai and the Care and Use of Bonsai Tools.* Tokyo and San Francisco: Japan Publications, Inc., 1971.

Kobayashi, Norio. *Bonsai: Miniature Potted Trees.* Tokyo: Japan Travel Bureau, 1951.

Murata, Kenji. *Photographs of Famous Miniature Trees.* 10 vols. Tokyo: Koju-en Nursery, 1956.

———. *Practical Bonsai for Beginners.* New York and Tokyo: Japan Publications Trading Co., 1964.

Murata, Kyūzō. *Bonsai: Miniature Potted Trees.* How-to Series, no. 1. Tokyo: Shufuno-tomo Co., Ltd., 1964.

Naka, John Yoshio. *Bonsai Techniques.* Santa Monica, Cal.: published for the Bonsai Institute of California by Dennis-Landman, 1973.

Onuki, Chuzo. *Bonsai.* Tokyo: Jitsugyo no Nihon Sha Co. Ltd., 1964.

Perry, Lynn R. *Bonsai: Trees and Shrubs; A Guide to the Methods of Kyuzo Murata.* New York: The Ronald Press Co., 1964.

Reader's Digest. *Complete Book of the Garden.* Pleasantville, N.Y.: Reader's Digest Association, 1966.

Stowell, Jerald P. *Bonsai: Indoors and Out.* Princeton, N.J.: D. Van Nostrand Company, Inc., 1966.

Tukey, Harold B. *Dwarfed Fruit Trees.* New York: The MacMillan Company, 1964.

U. S., Department of Agriculture, Forest Service. "Mycorrhizae," *Proceedings of the First North American Conference on Mycorrhizae, April, 1969.* Misc. Publication 1189. Washington: U. S. Government Printing Office, 1971.

Valavanis, William N. "Japanese Five-needle Pine," *Encyclopedia of Classical Bonsai Art.* Atlanta, Ga.: Symmes Systems, 1976.

Yoshimura, Yuji, and Halford, Giovanna M. *The Japanese Art of Miniature Trees and Landscapes.* Rutland, Vt. and Tokyo: Charles E. Tuttle Co., 1957.

INDEX

Plants are listed here by common name when they are the only representative of their genera; otherwise, they are listed by genus. If you wanted to refer to American elm, for example, you would find no entry; but the entry "elm" informs you that all elms are listed under *"Ulmus,"* where you will find the entry for American elm.

Italic numbers refer to the illustrations.

Abies (fir), 22, 76
   A. firma, Japanese f., 123
   A. lasiocarpa, alpine f., 16, 105, 123
   A. sachalinensis, Sakhalin f., 123
accessory plants, 108–9; *40, 49, 54, 55, 59, 74, 75*
Acer (maple), 58, 63, 64, 78, 93, 95, 96, 101, 104, 105, 120
   A. buergerianum, trident m., 17, 29, 125–26
   A. ginnala, hedge m., *81, 82*
   A. palmatum, Japanese m., 92, 126; *22*
   A. palmatum dissectum, cut-leaf m., 126
   A. rubrum, red m., 16–17, 29, 125–26
Acrous pusillus, 55, 59, 62, 63, 64
air circulation, 57
alpine buttercup, *Ranunculus eschscholtzii,* 108
Amelanchier (serviceberry), 62, 77, 97, 120, 127
   A. asiatica, Japanese s., 127
American bald cypress, *Taxodium distichum,* 16, 76, 98, 124
American Bonsai Society, 114, 115

American columbine, *Aquilegia canadensis,* 109
apex, 78
aphids, treatment for, 65–66
apple. *See Malus*
apricot. *See Prunus*
Arnold Arboretum, 115
art, defined, 18
azalea. *See Rhododendron*

balance, defined, 19–20
banyan tree, *Ficus benghalensis,* 100
barberry, *Berberis* spp., 62, 93, 120
beech. *See Fagus*
Benomyl, 66; *104*
Betula (birch), 64, 76, 78, 93
   B. nigra, river b., 128–29
   B. papyrifera, paper b., 97, 128–29
   B. platyphylla var. *japonica,* Japanese white b., 128–29
   B. populifolia, gray b., 128–29
bittersweet, *Celastrus scandens,* 62, 78, 86
black locust, *Robinia pseudoacacia,* 22; *5*
black olive, *Bucida buceras,* 100
blueberry, *Vaccinium* spp., 78, 86
blue-eyed grass, *Sisyrinchium* spp., 109
bluet, *Houstonia caerulea,* 109
bog rosemary, *Andromeda polifolia* cvs., 129–30
Bonide, 82; *104*
bonsai. *See also* collected material; collecting
   benches, *87–90*

developing bonsai, 31–33, 36; *27–35*
Diospyros (persimmon)
  D. kaki, Japanese p., 131
  D. lotus, date plum, 131
  D. virginiana, American p., 131
displaying bonsai
  bases for, 107–8
  indoors, 107–8
  outdoors, 109–10; *126*
dogwood, *Cornus* spp., 63
Douglas fir, *Pseudotsuga taxifolia,* 125
downy rattlesnake plantain, *Goodyera pubescens,* 109
drainage, 74
Duke Gardens Foundations, Inc., 115
dwarf bamboo, 93
dwarf crested iris, *Iris cristata, 49, 74*
dwarfed material, 21, 78, 85
dwarf *hinoki, Chamaecyparis obtusa nana,* 124
dwarf winged-bark euonymous, *Euonymous alata compacta,* 93, 97

eastern red cedar. *See Juniperus virginiana*
elm. *See Ulmus*
emphasis, defined, 20
English ivy, *Hedera helix,* 93, 99, 120, 130; *57, 62*
Enkianthus (enkianthus)
  E. campanalatus, e., 106
  E. cernus, e., 130
  E. perulatus, e., 130
exhibiting, 110–13; *127, 128. See also* judging

Fagus (beech), 76, 78, 93, 95, 120, 121
  F. crenata, Japanese b. (*buna*), 14, 129
  F. grandifolia, American b., 86, 129
  F. sylvatica, European b., 105, 129
false cypress. *See Chamaecyparis*
fern. *See* Christmas fern
fertilizers, *93*
  elements of, *57*
  types of, *57–58*
  using, *57–58; 94, 95*
fir. *See Abies*
forest style, *20–22, 58*
form, defined, 18
formal upright style, 21, 22–23, 32, 113; *13–15, 52, 53, 80*
forsythia, *Forsythia* spp., 92, 97
front (of bonsai), 32, 113–14
fungicide, 66, 82

Gardenia (gardenia), 92, 99, 120, 121
  G. jasminoides, cape jasmine, 130–31
  G. jasminoides var. *radicans,* g., 130–31; *55*
George Landis Arboretum, 115
geranium, *Pelargonium* sp., *57*
ginkgo, *Ginkgo biloba,* 93, 105, 120, 126
golden willow, 93
gold-star grass, *Hypoxis hirsuta,* 109
grass planting, *50*
greenhouse, *92*
growing regions, 94, 122. *See also* regions by name

hackberry. *See Celtis*
Hamamelis (witch hazel)
  H. japonica, Japanese w. h., 127
  H. vernalis, common w. h., 127
  H. virginiana, southern w. h., 127
hawthorn. *See Crateagus*
heath, *Erica* spp., 130
heather, *Calluna* spp., 130
hemlock. *See Tsuga*
hickory, *Carya* sp., 6
hinoki, Chamaecyparis obtusa, 99, 124
holly. *See Ilex*
honey locust, *Gleditsia triacanthos,* 128
honeysuckle, *Lonicera* spp., 62–63
hop hornbeam, *Ostrya virginiana,* 129
hornbeam. *See Carpinus*
horsetail, *Equisetum* spp., 109
humus, 74

Ilex (holly), 93, 96, 120, 121
  I. serrata, Japanese deciduous h. (*umemodoki*), 17, 88, 95
  I. verticillata, winterberry or black alder, 17, 77, 78, 88
informal upright style, 21, 22–24, 113; *16, 44–46, 59–61, 65–69, 71, 76–78, 81–86*
insecticide, 66, 82

Japanese Art of Miniature Trees and Shrubs, The (Yoshimura and Halford), 27, 113
Japanese gray-bark elm, *Zelkova serrata,* 120, 126
Japanese snowbell, *Styrax japonica,* 127
Japanese stewartia, *Stewartia pseudocamellia maxim,* 106, 130
Jasminum (jasmine), 92, 99. *See also* cape j.; star j.
  J. nitidum, confederate j., 131
  J. nudiflorum, winter j., 120, 131
  J. officinale, poet's j., 131

star jasmine, *Trachelospermum jasminoides,* 99

styles, 21, 32, 113. *See also bunjin;* cascade; forest; formal upright; informal upright; multiple trunk; rock planting; semicascade; tray landscape; twin trunk; twin trunk informal upright; wind-swept

sugarberry, *Celtis laevigata,* 99

suiseki, defined, 13

sunlight, requirements for, 40, 57, 82

surface roots, aesthetics of, 27–28, 31

sweet gum, *Liquidambar styraciflua,* 99, 102, 105, 127

sweet olive, 92

tamarisk, *Tamarix parviflora,* 93, 102

Taxus (yew), 104, 120
    T. baccata, English y., 125
    T. cuspidata, Japanese y., 125

temperature extremes, 118–19. *See also* regions by name

Terra-Green, 73

texture, defined, 19

tokonoma, 107

trailing arbutus, *Epigaea repens,* 109

tray landscape style, *49, 74*

trimming. *See* pruning

trunk, 21–22, 31

Tsuga (hemlock), 76, 78, 106, 120, 121
    T. canadensis, eastern h., 87, 97, 125
    T. diversifolia, northern h., 125
    T. heterophylla, western h., 87
    T. sieboldii, Japanese h., 125

Turf-Face, 73

twin trunk style, *24, 56, 72*

twin trunk informal upright style, *51*

Ulmus (elm), 58, 63, 64, 101, 105, 120, 121; *9. See also* Japanese gray-bark e.
    U. alata, winged e., 126
    U. americana, American e., 126; *56, 66*
    U. crassifolia, cedar e., 16, 126; *16*

U. parviflora, Chinese e., 93, 97
U. pumila, Siberian e., 126

unity, defined, 20

U. S. National Arboretum, 115

Viola (violet)
    V. pedata, bird's-foot v., 109
    V. rotundifolia, yellow v., 109
    V. sororio, blue v., 109

Virginia creeper, *Parthenocissus quinquefolia,* 97

Virginia saxifrage, *Saxifraga virginiensis,* 109

water, importance of, 70

watering
    after potting, 38
    how to do, 39–40; *36*
    willow and wisteria, 40

"water stone," defined, 13

wax myrtle, *Myrica cerifera, 3*

wax tree, *Rhus succedanea,* 126

Waylite, 73, 74

weeping willow; willow. *See Salix*

wind-swept style, *40, 73*

winterberry. *See Ilex*

winter care, 66–68, 81. *See also* regions by name

wintergreen, *Gaultheria procumbens,* 109; *75*

winter hazel, *Corylopsis spicata,* 129

winter sweet, *Spiraea* spp., 92

wiring
    branches, 23, 36–37
    gauges of wire for, 33, 36; *25*
    schedule, 121

Wisteria (wisteria), 40, 92, 120, 121; *123*
    W. floribunda, Japanese w., 132
    W. sinensis, Chinese w., 99, 132

witch hazel. *See Hamamelis*

woodland aster, *Aster divaricatus,* 109; *40, 62, 64*

yew. *See Taxus*

Zelkova serrata, Japanese gray-bark elm, 120, 126